Too Quick Despairer

Too Quick Despairer

A Life of Arthur Hugh Clough

David Williams

Rupert Hart-Davis   LONDON   1969

© David Williams 1969
First published 1969
Rupert Hart-Davis Ltd
3 Upper James Street
Golden Square, London W1

Printed in Great Britain by
The Garden City Press Ltd
Letchworth, Hertfordshire

SBN: 246 98566 6

Illustrations

One

ON Sunday mornings in the spring of 1826 a sedate little party
could be seen picking its way through the dusty streets of Charleston, South Carolina, heading for the Anglican church of St
Michael's. There were three young children in the group—
Arthur Hugh, aged seven, Anne Jemima, aged six, and George
Augustus, aged five. The shepherding mother was a tall, dignified,
strikingly handsome young woman possessed of dark hair and eyes
and a complexion which remained delicate in spite of the fierce sun
and the clear skies. The children were quiet, well-behaved, and
stared hard at everything. These excursions now afforded them
almost their only chance of walking abroad and leaving their
large, ugly, red-brick house on East Bay, from the windows of
which they could see the ships sailing in and out of the harbour.
The mother seemed anxious and depressed. Her husband had set
sail for England some while since, and she hated the long, weary
months when he was obliged to leave her in order to attend to
the English side of his business in Liverpool. She too was rarely
to be seen in the town except during this weekly journey to St
Michael's.

St Michael's was old; old, that is, by Charleston standards. It
had been built before the Revolution and the spire was sizeable
enough to remind you of a London church. A large porch ran
along its whole width and here, at about the time for service, the
men used to gather. The women and children had to push through
them and make their way to their particular pews. The men would
drift in later or perhaps not at all. There were stools at the corners
of the pews for the young children and pretty books for them to

7

look at when Bishop Bowen proved too long or too tedious. There was even room for the very tiny ones to be laid down and put to sleep.

In the aisles the slaves stood or crouched. Mrs Clough and her husband owned no Negroes, though their servants were of course slaves whom they had hired. She kept her eyes averted from them as she made her way to her pew. Slavery was a painful subject and troublesome to her evangelical conscience. She remembered too the incident of the runaway slave who had been harboured by one of the women-servants of her household. James her husband, far away in England now and so much missed, had been put to great trouble to get her flogging commuted to a fortnight's spell on the treadmill.

Mrs Clough knew nobody, seemed not to want to know anybody. She kept herself shut up in the redbrick house all week, nerved herself for the Sunday sortie through the unpaved streets of this savage, foreign place, dreamed of the return of James, and wrapped herself up in her children, now settled silent and submissive in the pew. The children were her comfort and joy, especially Arthur who was the eldest at home now that Charles, born in 1817, had been taken to England by his father in order to begin his education.

Arthur was receptive and intelligent. Mrs Clough looked at him fondly, hoping that he would remember, when it came to the public prayers, to substitute for 'the President' 'the King'. The Cloughs were English and she was determined that her children should be given a sense of this, although for the time being they were condemned to live amongst unsuitable foreigners. That was why she had never countenanced the idea of their going to school in Charleston. They must play amongst themselves and be discouraged from making friends with the local children. And as for their education, she would be reponsible for that herself, at any rate until the boys were old enough to go to England. Mrs Clough was grateful for this task which she had undertaken. Making a start on the boys' education gave her something to do; it also provided her with an excuse for monopolising Arthur. Mrs Clough was a woman with only a small gift for friendship. It was because of this that the attachments she did form tended to be close. Her attachment to Arthur, especially now that her husband and the eldest boy Charles were beyond the seas, was not so much close as

8

stifling. 'She poured out the fulness of her heart on him'—that was how Anne Jemima, writing thirty-five years later, described the relationship.

Mrs Clough had been born Ann Perfect, the daughter of a banker in Pontefract, Yorkshire. She was a clinging, complicated person. She needed companionship but was always averse to going out and looking for it. She wanted affection and, in a very restricted circle—not much more numerous than her own family and her closest relations—was ready to give it. But to give it, as it were, in secret. Anything like a parade or a demonstration was, even in private, beyond her. It was from the father, James Butler Clough, gayer, more energetic, more sanguine, less turned in upon himself, that the children received the outward and visible signs of affection which in most families it is the mother's delight to give—and perhaps give over-abundantly. Mrs Clough was indolent, slow always to see any necessity to be up and doing. Anne Jemima, who was to travel far from the security of the little stool in the shut-in pew of St Michael's and become the first principal of Newnham College, Cambridge, wrote of her mother: 'She was at all times of her life content to spend much of her time sitting at home with a book.'

But although she was clinging and missed her husband when he went away, more intensely perhaps than was healthy, although she kept her children too close to her, making them recipients of a deep, inarticulate devotion which could not fail to have been wholly bad for them, she was none the less exceptionally intelligent and not without her share of Yorkshire hard-headedness. She admired her husband and when she taught the children—she could be an inspiring teacher—she gave plentiful time to the greatness of the Clough family. Arthur, an attractive child 'with soft, silky, almost black hair, and shining dark eyes, and a small, delicate mouth', used to be told about Sir Richard Clough, Antwerp merchant and agent of Sir Thomas Gresham, founder of the Royal Exchange, and about the Clough relationship with John Calvin and even, more distantly, with the Welsh Tudors. But although she admired her husband she could see he was not really suited to the business career he had chosen. (James Butler Clough, with the insouciant enterprise characteristic of him, had left the family home in Denbighshire and gone into business as a cotton merchant in Liverpool, where he and Ann Perfect had been married in 1816.) It was not for her, a woman, to tell him how to avoid mistakes in business, but there can be little doubt that she possessed the shrewdness which, had it been made use of, would have kept the Clough cotton business clear of the troubles which were lying in wait for it. Sometimes this strain in her was strong enough to override the wifely dutifulness which the 1820s expected of a woman and, instead of marching with him hand in hand, clear-eyed yet silently submissive, towards financial ruin, she would express open disapproval of the rashness of her husband's goings-on.

Her intelligence displayed itself clearly enough in the authority and compellingness which she brought to her teaching. She had read widely. Charleston had given her plenty of time for it. She read history and poetry and books on religion. Little Arthur learnt about her heroes: about the great ones of the past who had unshrinkingly answered the calls of duty and conscience however uncomfortable or even dangerous, in the mere personal sense, those calls might have been. He learnt about Leonidas at Thermopylae and about Epaminondas who never shirked the meanest of duties if it was the well-being of his country which required them of him. He learnt about the Protestant martyrs. He had the loving-kindness of his earthly father dinned into him and, *a fortiori*, the loving-kindness of his Father in Heaven which was as valid, did he perhaps suppose? for those black men squatting in the aisles as for himself snug on his stool in the pew and listening, on and off, to the slow unfolding of Bishop Bowen's homily as it rolled over him.

As the spring gave way to summer and the sun beat more strongly down on the redbrick house and on the breakwater's white walls made of oyster shells beaten fine and hard, preparations were made for evacuating Charleston. The summer heat there was thought to be altogether too much for young children and for a Yorkshire Perfect possessed of a delicate complexion. These seasonal migrations were something the children much looked forward to. They enlarged their freedom not only because of the journeys themselves but because, once settled in the new temporary abodes their lives were much less circumscribed. In Charleston no roaming abroad was ever allowed. English children, in Mrs Clough's view, were to be protected in such a half-civilised tropical place from the dangers which might come from fraternisation. True the Calders and the Bulleys lived there, exiles like themselves from Liverpool, though even here Mrs Clough was slow to make friends. For Arthur and Anne and George the Sunday morning turn-out to St Michael's was the central excitement of the week. It gave them the chance to study people at closer range and to watch them going about their business. Apart from Sunday mornings their only brush with the outside world was on Saturdays when the men drove to market and the children went with them. For the rest of the week it was the redbrick house on East Bay, and lessons with mother, and hour-long starings out of the nursery windows at the ships sailing in and out of the harbour, and descents for more strenuous games to the lower storey where James Clough had his office and where piles of cotton lay about on the warehouse floor.

The move to summer quarters meant a change from all this. Arthur, now seven years old, could remember earlier ones: the sea-route holiday to New York, for example, when he was four. He could still picture the boarding-house they had stayed in and after that a comfortable house belonging to some friend of his father's where they had lived for a while. There had been a large garden, he remembered, which ran down to the banks of the Hudson River. It was there that for the first time he had suddenly found himself able to read. And the following summer they had sailed for New York again and had stayed at Albany and Lebanon Springs, and thirty years later he wrote of 'long years ago seeing... birches on a hill near Lebanon Springs, up which we children were taken to look out over a tract of country which we were told was Massachusetts'.

This summer of 1826 there was not to be so much travelling. For Mrs Clough, for the time being a lone woman with young children, somewhere close at hand had to be found. They were to go to Sullivan's Island. For Arthur, his imagination already stirred by storybooks of his own reading and by Prescott's *Conquest of Peru* and by Washington Irving's *Life of Columbus* read to him by his mother, the place sounded full of promise.

A child can quickly build a sizeable fairyland out of a couple of words, and suffer inarticulate frustration and disappointment once time has moved on and changed those two words into unsatisfactory reality. Sullivan's Island was not like that. It sounded good in prospect and it was good when they had got there. It lay a few miles off the coast from Charleston and was 'like one great sandbank'. Where the Cloughs lived there were few inhabitants; it was judged safe for the children to roam. They could paddle and listen to the screaming of the innumerable curlews. They could go down to the shore on the first days and watch the sailing ship come in from Charleston, bringing their chattels from the redbrick house and depositing them on the sand. There were sudden violent storms to enjoy too, and occasional shipwrecks to be thrilled about. Once, in a storm, it looked as though their wooden cottage on the shore was going to be engulfed by the waves; it was saved only by a last-minute change in the direction of the wind. Arthur, cloistered and fastidious and too much worked upon by his mother, enjoyed it all but with much less abandon than the other two. When they walked along the beach he refused to take off his shoes and stockings. He was an obstinate boy. When they played Swiss Family Robinson together, he was always chosen for, or chose for himself, the part of Ernest. Arthur Hugh Clough was not, at any period of his life, very much of an actor. Ernest was a part he could play without doing any violence to his personality. Undoubtedly he enjoyed his holidays, though it is from his sister, Anne Jemima, that most of the colourful details come about those days on Sullivan's Island. It is she who tells us about the hurricanes and the curlews. Arthur keeps it more to himself. But a few years later, one day when he was ill at Rugby and watching from his window the younger children of the great Doctor at their games, he was moved to write a poem to his headmaster and in it Sullivan's Island makes a shy, not too colourful appearance:

> *I looked upon thy children, and I thought of all and each,*
> *Of my brother and my sister, and our rambles on the beach,*
> *Of my mother's gentle voice, and my mother's beckoning hand,*
> *And all the tales she used to tell of the far, far English land.*

Sullivan's Island was still only abroad, a fact which Mrs Clough was at pains to keep firmly planted in the forefront of her children's minds.

For all that, Sullivan's Island was a success. They went there again in the summer of 1827. James Butler Clough was back by then. He returned in the late autumn of 1826. He started to teach Arthur Latin and arithmetic. Perhaps he felt it was time to introduce some variety into an intellectual diet composed of enthusiastic history and Protestant martyrdom.

Whatever his motives, the process by which Arthur was to be turned, within the space of a dozen years or so, into one of the finest classical scholars of his generation, was now modestly begun. The amount of personal influence a father exerts upon a son is always difficult to evaluate. In Arthur's case the strength of it certainly cannot have been overriding. They did not see enough of each other during the formative years. Arthur was never really given the chance either to imitate an admired senior or to turn upside down, in the conduct of his own life, the ways and manners of someone subconsciously loathed. In the sphere of personal influence it was Ann Perfect who counted. That of course did not stop Arthur from being the inheritor of some of his father's genes. Both of them were restless, for one thing. Neither of them was ever found wanting when it was a question of 'having a go'. And neither of them was easily turned from a course of action, however rash or inadvisable in terms of expediency, once decided upon.

The return of James Butler Clough from England meant also that Arthur could now begin to lead a healthier, less cloistered life. There was something more to do beside listen to mother, gaze listlessly out of the nursery windows on the upper floor at the traffic of the harbour and read the Waverley Novels or the travels of Captain Cook. His father had business to do down at the wharves and on board the anchored ships. Arthur was now old enough to accompany him. And James Butler Clough was sociable. He came from a long line of Welsh gentry who were accustomed to keeping open house at Plas Clough in Denbighshire. People began to drop in in the evenings once they knew that Mr Clough was back again from his visit to England. The captains of the merchantmen lying in the harbour would call on them and Arthur would listen to the conversation and the tall stories.

The summer of 1827 they again spent on Sullivan's Island which proved to be more enjoyable than ever, perhaps because of the volatile presence of father. The house they took there this time was large and rambling. It had a verandah and on this Mr Clough had a swing put up for the children. It was built in two blocks (it had begun as an inn). Mr and Mrs Clough slept in a room over a large billiard room. This block was reached only by an open staircase or by a little open path across a roof. The frequent violent storms could be enjoyed this year with a greater sense of security than before because when they broke Mr Clough used to come for the children and carry them across the little open path into the parents' more sheltered block. Their walks became more adventurous. Sometimes they went as far as Fort Moultrie which was in those days a redbrick fort with a dry ditch surrounding it. A high ridge of sand lay between it and the sea and once the children had crossed this there were excitements in plenty for them immediately to hand: a desolate, deserted house half buried in sand, tall palmetto trees, some of them prostrate having been uprooted by high tides and hurricanes, and, further off still, a beautiful grove of myrtle trees. At the other end of the island you got sociability and bustle; a criss-cross pattern of steamers and sailing-boats on their way between the island and the city, a plentiful traffic of gigs and waggons, nearly all of them with a hood or an awning against the sun and with a high seat behind for the Negro boy. And always, save when a storm was on its way, the bay was populous with fishing-boats and rowing-boats.

In his sedate, too grown-up way Arthur enjoyed it, but did not retain the colourful details as firmly as his sister, perhaps because his thoughts were already turning to the long journey that lay ahead. Arthur was to follow his elder brother Charles to England. He was to go to a prep school in Chester where James Butler Clough's father now lived. It was a large, and perhaps daunting, prospect for a boy of eight to contemplate. He clung to the reassuring thought that he was not at any rate to face the journey alone. His father would be coming as well, as he had done in the case of brother Charles. But this time Mrs Clough was not to be left to pine and brood. The whole family would undertake the journey, make a round of visits to relations, and see Arthur settled in Chester before returning to America in October.

The Cloughs duly sailed from Charleston early in June 1828. They turned out to be the only children on board and were given the run of the ship. They were indulged by all the grown-ups partly because, being only three, they were not numerous enough ever to become a nuisance, and partly because, conditioned by the oppressive, shut-in uneventfulness of Mrs Clough's regime, they were not rumbustious children anyway. The voyage, inevitably long, would have stimulated most children into becoming so because there was so much for them to wonder at: the intricate, multifarious, day-to-day working of the ship itself, the tightly

14

interlaced rafts of seaweed they saw floating in the channel of the Gulf Stream, a waterspout to ask questions about, an iceberg, awe-inspiring but mercifully distant, and then at last, with the south of Ireland on the horizon, the creeping small boats of the Irish fishermen as they came out to trade in fresh fish. There were storms too, with father, venturesome and protective, always ready to take them up the companion-way for a peep at the great waves.

After docking at Liverpool came a round of visits to relations and the rediscovery of Charles, by this time thoroughly acclimatised to England. Arthur gave immediate signs that the acclimatising process was with him going to be long and painful. The swarming broods of cousins he was introduced to in Yorkshire and in Wales were at first altogether too much for him. The long, quiet communings with his mother at home in Charleston, and then, after James Butler's return from England, the snug luxuries of being monopolised by an affectionate and impetuous father—these were not at all an effective preparation for this new life: being pitchforked into households where cousins, ten to a dozen strong, swarmed and whooped. 'Arthur could not enter into the boys' rough games and amusements', his sister admits, but adds that as the months went by and the round of visits lengthened 'Arthur became more sociable'. He remembered those shrinking feelings of his when, not long before he died, he came to the writing of the First Lawyer's Tale in *Mari Magno*, and made his hero-narrator say:

> *I was not quite composed, I own,*
> *Except when with the girls alone;*
> *Looked to their father still with fear*
> *Of how to him I must appear;*
> *And was entirely put to shame,*
> *When once some rough, he-cousins came.*

The long, cross-country drives they made by coach—from Liverpool to Pontefract, for example, where the Perfects lived—kept them interested. And from Pontefract it wasn't far to York where the Minster, so much larger and grander than St Michael's back home, impressed them all. And now and then there was a visit which provided a welcome interval of recuperative calm. There was one which they particularly enjoyed—to Uncle Charles in his funny old vicarage in Mold. Uncle Charles was a bachelor

15

and lived alone. He was kind—even culpably indulgent, never minding the sliding and the slithering that took place over the shining oak floors of his vicarage. And there was another trip to the seaside near Colwyn Bay, which was a bit like Sullivan's Island, the children thought, only nicer.

The summer days began to shorten, and before long it was time for the final stop at Chester where Arthur was to stay with his grandfather and be broken in at a prep school before joining his brother Charles at Rugby in the following July. At no point in after life does he make much mention of this parting which must have been grievous. His sister is tight-lipped about it too, but contrives none the less a blankly poignant sentence. 'In October Arthur went to school at Chester, and my father, mother, George and I sailed again to Charleston. This was practically the end of Arthur's childhood.' To say goodbye to childhood with one's tenth birthday still nearly three months away strikes us as drastic. Perhaps to Arthur it came more easily than to most. At all events he makes a tolerably convincing display of elderliness in a letter which he writes to his sister in the spring of the following year, 1829. '...We have bought a book entitled *The Newtonian System of Philosophy* which treats chiefly on the power and weight of air...I was sorry to hear Mrs Roper had been so unwell and that Mr R. had lost that fine large dog Cora. The summer vacation is now fast approaching after which we shall be conducted by either Uncle Charles or Alfred to Rugby which is not far from Leamington... Were you not grieved to hear that magnificent building York Minster had been partly destroyed through the destructive means of fire? What a short time it appears since we saw that immense, vast and beautiful East Window, since we heard the sounds proceeding from that majestic organ, since we viewed those elegant arches now a heap of blackened ruins. I must now wish you goodbye, so with best love to Papa, Mama, and Georgy, believe to remain...' Reading it over the shoulder of Anne Jemima, his parents—and Ann Perfect Clough particularly—must have been consoled. Arthur seemed ready for Rugby.

Two

In July 1829 Thomas Arnold was almost as new a boy at Rugby as Arthur Hugh Clough. It was only eleven months before that he and his numerous family—Mary his wife, six children, two nurses and Miss Rutland—had driven up from Oxford on the second stage of their journey by coach from Laleham to take over the stewardship of the school from Dr John Wooll. 'It rained heartily,' Arnold noted in his diary for that day (August 6, 1828), 'a good part of the day, and Miss Rutland and the children were obliged to go within, where they must have had a rare stuffing, six children and two nurses and Miss Rutland all squeezed together.'

Then, as now, the public schools were coming in for criticism. Rugby, where Wooll had reigned for twenty-one years, was no better, and no worse, than the others. It differed from many of the old foundations however in that its trustees were more generous than most in the amount of rein they were disposed to give to their headmaster. The right to expel, for example, was one which Arnold had insisted upon before consenting that his name should go forward as a candidate for the appointment. 'Expulsion should be practised more often than it is,' he wrote. 'Now, I know that trustees, in general, are averse to this plan because it has a tendency to lessen the numbers of the school...Yet I could not consent to tolerate much that I know is tolerated already.'

'Much that is tolerated already'—what were the shortcomings and abuses upon which the English genius for toleration was being given a chance to exercise itself? Arnold, as thoroughly and as completely as anybody, was familiar with them. He had experienced them himself as a schoolboy at Winchester. Chief

17

perhaps was the lamentable inadequacy of the teaching staff. An usher, then as now, tended to be badly paid. But, as he was then usually in holy orders, opportunities for supplementing his stipend lay conveniently to hand. Curacies could be wangled and the ushers wangled them. The time they could give to their work as teachers had in consequence to be rationed. This meant that in a boarding school boys were left to themselves, unsupervised and undirected, for dangerously long stretches of time. If he is alone, or has a single congenial partner, the human boy can roam well clear of any taskmaster's eye for a long time and probably profit from the freedom. It is dangerous, though, as Mr William Golding has brilliantly demonstrated in *Lord of the Flies*, to leave a whole flock long without a shepherd.

And even when they were there the shepherds were not noticeably given to pastoral care. They entered their schoolrooms armed and at the ready, with bared teeth as it were and with minatory whip-crackings to accompany the raising of the door-latch. They were lion-tamers paying their daily, hated visit to the noisy, foul-smelling cage. Their pupils were, almost by definition, hostile and evilly disposed. Intimidation was the only treatment which stood any chance of proving effective. The ushers flogged. They flogged sleepiness or incomprehension as mercilessly as insolence or rowdyism. Dr Wooll, a decent, agreeable man enough, once flogged thirty-eight boys in fifteen minutes. He did it because he thought that that was what a boy needed. Did they have memories, these pre-Arnoldian schoolmasters—the Woolls and the Keates, the Gabells and the Goddards? Did they remember their own terrors, the horsewhippings and the raw backsides of their own childhood? And didn't it ever occur to any single one of them that now at last it lay in their power to make a change? Apparently it didn't. The wall between childhood and manhood is high and almost unscaleable, and every added year seems to put one more course on the brickwork. Flesh wounds skin over too, and the scar tissue is tough and insensitive.

So it was to this question of the ushers that Thomas Arnold gave his first thoughts. What must he do to improve the quality and increase the co-operativeness of his staff? He was ready with the practical answer. He must raise their salaries, and he had the means to do this because, with the plan already in his mind, he had persuaded the trustees, more than three months before taking up his appointment, to increase the amount of the fees charged to pupils. They were to go up from thirty to fifty guineas a half for non-foundationers and from five to twelve for the scholars. 'I went down to Rugby,' he writes to J. T. Coleridge on April 28, 1828, 'a fortnight since, to meet the trustees. The terms of the school, which were far too low'—England had not, by 1828, finished with post-war inflation—'have been raised on my representation.' In 1829 Rugby masters began to earn the very handsome salary of £500 a year. Arnold had now the right to require them to relinquish their curacies and to give themselves wholly, and wholeheartedly, to the duties of schoolmastering as he conceived them.

Another of the criticisms which the public schools of the twenties of the last century were being asked, particularly in the Whig press, to answer was the still familiar one of narrowness of curriculum. Latin and Greek, Greek and Latin, the school day began, continued and ended with these. But this was never, either at the beginning or afterwards, an issue which caused Arnold's eyes to flash or kindled his reformist zeal. A few meagre side dishes were on offer at Rugby during his time but the bully beef of classical syntax continued to provide the bulk and substance of the diet. And perhaps on this score his schoolmasterly instincts were not as extravagantly at fault as present-day trends in curriculum-devising might lead one to suppose. The first, and indeed the only really important, question to be asked when the matter of the training and enrichment of young minds is to be considered is not What is being taught? but, Who is doing the teaching?

And in any case academic prowess, classical or other, was never for Arnold the justification of any school's existence. He would have refused to be impressed by a school such as, say, St Paul's as it was sixty years later under F. W. Walker who looked upon an open scholarship in classics to Trinity or Balliol as the ultimate dazzling crown at which all civilised schoolmasterly effort must always be grasping. Arnold's deepest admiration was kept for the boy who, by constant application and high-minded diligence, made the most of the meagre talents he had been born with. If a boy was brilliant into the bargain—as Clough was, or Stanley was, or Lake—why, that was an agreeable piece of good fortune for him. But the brilliance was never, in itself, the thing that mattered

19

for Arnold. What mattered was the boy's management of himself, the control, both inward and outward, which he was able to exercise on his resources. 'Conduct', in fact, to quote a famous remark made by his greatest son, 'is three fourths of life.'

How was he to make boys behave themselves well? This was the question which Arnold, with his intense dynamism and his confident certainties, tried primarily to answer. And he never made the mistake of thinking the question was other than tricky and tough. Boys were wild animals—so far the new young headmaster saw eye to eye with Wooll and Keate and with the Gabells and Goddards of his own school days at Winchester. But he knew also something of which those others seemed to be entirely unaware: that boys, again like wild animals, are extremely imitative, and that the unspoken but clearly deducible exhortation 'Don't do as I do. Do as I say' is the one which is always at all times absolutely certain to fail with them.

It was this knowledge, this certainty, which prompted him, as a first measure, to stimulate the co-operativeness of his staff and to appoint almost immediately two such young enthusiasts as Bonamy Price and James Prince Lee. But another reformist instrument, even more potent and effective, lay to his hand. The senior boys in the public boarding schools had always, inevitably, exercised considerable power. From above they were largely unsupervised and unguided. Towards their inferiors in age and strength they were free to act with all the caprice and autocratic inventiveness of Ivan the Terrible. Arnold brought all his guns—a very far from negligible armament—to bear on the praepostors. The privileges which they had always enjoyed were not to be taken away from them. Indeed they were to be increased much as the assistant masters' salaries had been increased. But now, as well as privileges, there were to be responsibilities. If the praepostors were to be treated as men—and Arnold was always careful to treat them so—they were to act as men, willing to observe in their own conduct, the rules of the establishment of which they were members and ready also to enforce upon the others, less fortunate, less mature, the scrupulous observance of those same rules. He had them to dine with him, four by four, every week and talked to them man to man, leaving the water-wings of his authority behind in the dressing-room upstairs. The effect of his powerful, mature personality was enormous. Some, no doubt, there were who proved unresponsive, but on the impressionable ones, the willing ones—and most boys are impressionable and willing—his influence was monopolistic and had almost the quality of hypnosis. The good conduct of the school was in their hands. 'What we must look for here,' he used to tell them, 'is, first, religious and moral principles, secondly, gentlemanly conduct and, thirdly, intellectual ability.'

Religious and moral principles. These must pervade his praepostors'—his agents'—lives. They must loom, unspoken but none the less paramount, behind the declensions and the paradigms and the ablative absolutes. And they must be his, the headmaster's, primary concern. And where could they be implanted most directly, most tellingly? Arnold had no doubt whatever about how this question should be answered. They could be expounded and illuminated best in his own sermons in his own school chapel—in that Rugby chapel which Matthew, his eldest son, though unable to share his father's confident Christianity, was yet most movingly to commemorate. In the *Apologia* Newman is moved to wonder whether Thomas Arnold was a Christian at all. And probably in Newman's sense he wasn't. For Newman Christianity was a matter of proclaiming oneself as entirely committed to a massive and complicated body of doctrine laid down and expounded by holy church; for Arnold the intricacies of any credal statement had little importance. 'Our Church now has a strict bond in matters of opinion,' he writes to J. T. Coleridge on November 18, 1835, 'and none at all in matters of practice; which seems to me a double error.' 'Matters of practice'—these were what counted for Arnold. Conduct, once again, is three fourths of life. Lytton Strachey, in his undeservedly famous essay on Dr Arnold in *Eminent Victorians*, makes much of the look of puzzlement which he claims to detect in the great headmaster's eyes, and giggles delightedly on discovering that Arnold should feel the need of a little spell in bed after a week-end of ding-dong theological argument with the tractarian W. G. Ward. Strachey's talent for being clever and silly at the same time is nowhere better illustrated than in his portrait of Arnold. No man of his generation was surer of himself than Arnold and less inclined to puzzled uncertainty. He went to bed to recover from Ward's visit not because Ward's sword had found a crack in the breastplate of his righteousness, but because of his distress resulting from a prolonged contemplation of a man of Ward's brilliance wasting his talents and his energies on causes which, if not lost, were at best scarcely important enough to be worth winning. 'One who had no misgivings'—that is Thomas Hughes' description of him in *Tom Brown's Schooldays*. 'Zealous, beneficent, *firm*'—that is how his son Matthew sums him up in 'Rugby Chapel'. No one could possibly have moulded, shaped and influenced boys and youths with Arnold's completeness and absolute sureness of touch without being in himself a personality quite brimming over with certainties. The hesitant man, the man with an itch to qualify, the man who would like notice of the question—or twenty-four hours, perhaps to think it over—has never in all history been the sort that boys and youths will accept as leader. They want a man who has no doubts. The merest whiff of hesitation, of self-mistrust, rises straight to their nostrils and turns them away.

It must not of course be imagined that the ten-year-old Arthur Hugh Clough became immediately aware of the formidable person who was to have control, either indirect or direct, over his life for the next eight years, and who was to influence him, for good or for ill, much more strongly and decisively than any other human being all his short life through. Arnold concentrated his direct attentions on his sixth formers; to the small boys he was a remote and awe-inspiring figure. There were of course the sermons to listen to and partially to comprehend, but even these were not as frequent in the early days of his headmastership as they were to become later. This is not to say that Arnold took no trouble over the younger end. He did. He watched them closely, and he knew all about them. But the boys themselves were not to be aware of this. For Clough at the beginning he could not have been more than an august dispenser of prizes or of general reproof. The letters home which have been preserved from those early Rugby days are few. Here, in a letter to his mother written in May 1830 after he had been upwards of nine months at Rugby, he shows a typical small boy's uncritical acceptance of administrative mishap, and introduces us to one who was to become a close sixth form friend and later to be Dean of Westminster as well as the first, and greatest, biographer of Arnold of Rugby. '…There was also another prize for boys in the fifth form which was gained by Stanley, for an English Essay "On Sicily and its Revolutions"…Stanley, who is not much bigger than Charley, came forth and read his Essay…

Unfortunately, the prizes had not arrived and therefore Dr Arnold was obliged to postpone the delivery of them for some time.'

Stanley, even at this early stage, was clearly showing promise. But Clough had never in his letters to content himself with noting down the prizewinning performances of others. He was clever and he was hardworking. All the way through he was able to earn the unqualified approval of his schoolmasters—that accolade which in later life so often turns out to be a kiss of death. He gained the only open scholarship then existing for boys of the school under fourteen years of age. At fifteen he was top of the fifth form, and at this point had to mark time for almost a year as no one was admitted to the sixth under the age of sixteen. During that waiting year he showed himself already aware of the responsibilities shortly to be placed upon him and of the many cleaning-up tasks still to be done at Rugby even after six full years of Arnold's tenure as headmaster. He wrote to his brother George now languishing unhappily at King William's College, Isle of Man, on October 13, 1834: '...I believe that King William's College is worse than many places, but even here at Rugby, the best of all public schools—even here there is a vast deal of bad. It was but a few nights ago that a little fellow not more than thirteen years old at the very most was quite drunk and that for the second time in the last year.' And again to George, who had not ceased complaining, a month later: ' "Fear not them that kill the body and after that have no more they can do, but rather fear Him who is able to destroy both Soul and Body in Hell." These words are some of them what Dr Arnold told us a long time since when I was like you "passing" my second year I fancy at a large School, where wickedness, yes, theft and drunkenness, were by no means uncommon, the latter indeed an everyday matter.'

At last in 1835 he entered the sixth form and became at once the model schoolboy to end all model schoolboys, the preposterous praepostor, the pathetically striving do-gooder with the weak ankles whom Lytton Strachey thought so funny, the over-virtuous paragon labouring devotedly in the eye of his great taskmaster Dr Arnold. A note of febrile surexcitation begins to be sounded in his letters, an hysterica passio which he is himself by no means wholly unaware of. Right at the beginning, in July 1835, he writes to his mother: 'I have been in one continued state of excitement for at least the last three years, and now comes the time of exhaustion.' And to his brother George in October of the same year: 'Simpkinson [one of his greatest friends at school] left me last Monday for Cambridge, and his absence has made me head of the school house, which is an office of considerable trust and great difficulty. Indeed you could not do better than try to win the liking and esteem of your school-fellows by being as kind to them as you can. I hope I am trying earnestly to do the same. But there is one danger in this occupation which assails *me*, at least, very often; and that is, the danger of carrying our wish too far.' But despite the brakes which he tried to put on himself the excitement of it all did carry him away, the missionary fervour aroused in him by his leadership of the select coterie of Arnold's disciples, by his 'living', as he put it, 'under and gathering wisdom from a great and good man' finally stifled any self-questionings he might have had about the dangers of over-enthusiasm. He would be the Galahad of the 'High Arnold set' (his own phrase) and, bemused by the magnificence of this conception, he wrote again, half defiantly, half pathetically, to Simpkinson in January 1836. 'I verily believe my whole being is soaked through with the wishing and hoping and striving to do the school good, or rather to keep it up and hinder it from falling in this, I do think, very critical time, so that all my cares and affections and conversations, thoughts, words and deeds, look to that involuntarily. I am afraid you will be inclined to think this "cant", and I am conscious that even one's truest feelings, if very frequently put out in the light, do make a bad and disagreeable appearance...'

Why does all the world dislike a prig? Chiefly, one must suppose, because the spectacle of virtue so spectacularly triumphant is in its nature so improbable that no reasonable man can be blamed for rooting around in search of the mirrors that have foisted the illusion on him. If, in fact, you are too good you can't be true. And if you are too good there is a slimy, self-seeking motive for it somewhere however artfully concealed by sanctimoniousness and the singing of anthems. But if to be a prig is to be, if only to the tiniest degree, a phoney, then Clough, even at his most exhortatory, even when he was fulsomely preachifying at poor George, young and lonely and unhappy in the barbarous Isle of Man, was no prig. He was himself much too young, and much too innocent, to strike an attitude, to roll his eyes heavenward in the interests of personal profit or personal advantage. Clough was not being a prig, or indeed anything else which implies any degree of deliberateness. Much more nearly he was for the time being a young fellow in a trance, an ardent being who had suffered temporary depersonalisation. In the words which Stanley wrote long afterwards, Clough, when he entered Arnold's sixth form at Rugby, 'received into an unusually susceptible and eager mind the whole force of that electric shock which Arnold communicated to all his better pupils.'

That susceptibility was made stronger than it otherwise might have been through two considerations: first, he was his mother's son and second he had had no home to go to in the holidays. A certain brooding intensity—lethargic in the mother's case, more restless and energetic in the son's—is characteristic of both of them. It is to be clearly seen in the spirit of absolute dedication which Clough brought to his self-chosen role as Arnold's standard-bearer. On November 9, 1835, he wrote to J. P. Gell: 'I don't know which to think the greatest, the blessing of being under Arnold, or the curse of being without a home.' True, he had various relations who never showed any lack of friendship or kindliness towards him, and in the holidays he used to go the rounds. He was particularly fond of the old bachelor in his vicarage at Mold—he writes to Anne in April 1834 of his 'predilection for the Vicarage at Mold, and moreover for living two in a house...Two is my favourite number. And by the by it would [be] no bad thing for [sic] you and I in some future time were to live together in some quiet Vicarage, if so be that I ever get one, or even here at Rugby, as a master; and this last life is one I should have no objection to at all provided we had a man anything like Arnold for our head.' But going the rounds was no substitute for going home. He had nowhere permanent, unchanging, shabby and relaxed to set against the feverish intensities of his life at Rugby, first as a star scholar and then as Arnold's permanent under-secretary for moral affairs. He had no home port where he could drop anchor and swing lazily up and down for a spell after a term of sailing before the high winds of Arnoldian doctrine. The memory of his deprivation was bitter even after a gap of nearly twenty years as this letter, written in February 1852 to Blanche Smith, his future wife, shows: 'I may perhaps be idle now; but when I was a boy, between fourteen and twenty-two throughout,

I may say, you don't know how much regular drudgery I went through. Holidays after holidays, when I was at school, after a week or so of recreation, which rarely came in an enjoyable form to me, the whole remaining five or six weeks I used to give to regular work at fixed hours. That wasn't so very easy for a school-boy, spending holidays, not at home, but with uncles, aunts, and cousins...Certainly, as a boy, I had less of boyish enjoyment of any kind whatever, either at home or at school, than nine-tenths of boys, at any rate of boys who go to school, college, and the like...'

The school's nickname for him was 'Tom Yankee', and it was always as 'Tom Yankee' that he signed his contributions to the *Rugby Magazine*. There is this contribution, for example, which, God knows, is schoolboyish enough but which is at any rate honest and which shows him stretching out his hands with love and longing to the infinitely distant redbrick house on East Bay, and the wooden cottage on Sullivan's Island where long, long ago a sedate small boy used to trudge with his sister through the white sand.

> *I used to think when I was there that my own true home was here.*
> *But home is not in land or sky, but in those whom each holds dear.*
> *The evening's cooling breeze is fanning my temples now,*
> *But then my frame was languid, and heated was my brow,*
> *And I longed for England's cool, and for England's breezes then,*
> *But now I would give full many a breeze to be back in the heat*
> *again.*

Not all his contributions to the *Rugby Magazine* are as inexpert as this (though some of them are worse, as when, an over-pressed young exile, he watches, from an upstairs sickroom window, the headmaster's children at play, and is moved to 'the happy, happy evening hours when I sat on my father's knee, / Oh! many a wave is rolling now betwixt that seat and me!') but all of them are honest, and try to express emotions genuinely felt. The magazine, incidentally, of which he was editor in 1835, was yet one more addition to the burdens he was carrying at this time.

I said he was lonely, and this is something which has to be stressed. He was lonely not only because his home was far away in South Carolina but because the friends at Rugby who meant most to him were older than he was and went on to the University a considerable while before he was old enough to follow them, leaving him with a latter-day Jehovah as his commanding officer, an overwhelming sense of mission, and no cronies to confide in. He wrote to Anne on October 10, 1835: 'My oldest and only friend Simpkinson is just gone to Cambridge; and there are also two or three more gone whom I knew and loved better than the rest; so that now I am quite alone, and am doomed so to remain for two long years.' And a month later the same complaint is heard in a letter to J. P. Gell, with a few additional words—the boy is much too besotted with devotion and much too intent upon following in the footsteps of the headmaster to realise that they are funny—on the activities which have to be made to compensate for the loss of such friends: '...I have to take care no less than you lest the excitement should carry me away; for though assuredly there is no Simpkinson here, or Vaughan, or Burbidge, yet it is most easy to find excitement on the one hand in fagging and on the other in associating with so many fellows for their good, which is a more dangerous employment than I looked for.'

So his life at School House went on, feverishly busy at three different levels all at the same time. First and pre-eminent were his responsibilities as head of School House. To him was entrusted the moral leadership, of him was required untiring vigilance. All the old familiar sins, ineradicable seemingly as thistle and charlock—sloth and drunkenness, sadism and homosexuality—were still lurking in the dark corners, ready to swagger into the open the instant the sentry left his box. But Clough was there, ready to wrestle and to overthrow, willing to exhort the tempted and the fainthearted just as, in hellfire pulpit prose, he exhorted poor little Georgy far away in the Isle of Man.

Next there was the tiring, demanding business of Do as I do, never do as I say. Athletics were good. They were a sort of therapeutic blotting paper designed to mop up tidily all the overflowing energies of youth; they could quieten the lusts of the flesh. Therefore Clough, in spite of much natural disinclination—physically his tendency always was to be slothful—would become an athlete. He did. He took a leading part in running, swimming and football. His name still stands in Rugby records as the first winner of the Barbey Hill run, and he is singled out in William Arnold's *Rules of Football* as the best goalkeeper on record—a high place which Tom Hughes, of *Tom Brown's Schooldays*, is similarly prepared to concede to him.

27

Public spiritedness too was an absolute good. How could Christian self-abnegation be preached, unless the question What can I do for Rugby? was made always to take precedence over the deplorable more familiar What can Rugby do for me? Therefore Clough would be public-spirited. He was. And evidence of this is perhaps most clearly seen in his strenuous labouring over the *Rugby Magazine*. Editing was of course much more congenial to him than goalkeeping, and he indulged himself to the extent of giving an immense amount of time to it and writing copiously for it as well. What he wrote was not on the whole more promising than the average run of shy, derivative commonplace which has filled thousands upon thousands of column inches in school magazines from his day to ours. It is easy to detect in his verses the haunting dread of moral backsliding implanted in him by Thomas Arnold:

> *The leaves were shining all about,*
> * You might almost have seen them springing;*
> *I heard the cuckoo's simple shout,*
> * And all the little birds were singing.*
> *It was not dull, the air was clear,*
> * All lovely sights and sounds to deal,*
> *My eyes could see, my ears could hear,*
> * Only my heart it would not feel;*
> *And yet that it should not be so,*
> * My mind kept telling me within;*
> *Though nought was wrong that I did know,*
> * I thought I must have done some sin.*

And it is easy too to see that Clough was as familiar as most with what Daddy Wordsworth could do on his off days:

> *Full soon my heart began to sink*
> * With a strange shame and inward pain,*
> *For I was sad within to think*
> * Of this absorbing love of gain,*
> *And various thoughts my bosom tost;*
> *When suddenly my path there crossed,*
> *Locked hand in hand with one another,*
> *A little maiden and her brother—*
> *A little maiden and she wore*
> *Around her waist a pinafore.*

But the main point here is not promise but performance. Clough performed. Dr Arnold expected public spirit and he should have it. He wrote to Georgy in September 1835: 'the magazine prospers; it will probably be out on the 1st October. "Egmont" will appear, and one or two other things of mine. I assure you I have enough to do. I sometimes think of giving up fagging hard here, and doing all my extra work in the holidays, as to have my time here free for these objects—1st. The improvement of the school; 2nd. The publication and telling abroad of the merits of the school by means of the magazine.'

And lastly, a long way after example and an even longer way after moral leadership, came his own personal concerns, his preoccupation about his studies and his future. He was to try for a Balliol scholarship, and by now it was becoming very important that he should be successful. James Butler Clough was discovering that to be sanguine and debonair was not enough to ensure success in business. A Balliol scholarship would bring honour and glory, and, equally important, though Clough hated having to think so, it would bring money. 'I shall not be very sorry to go to Oxford now,' he wrote to his mother in March 1838, 'for I find Stanley and Lake like it very much, and I daresay Dr Arnold will be a Bishop before very long. I only hope it may not be just yet. I must however do my very best to go there as I wish, namely with a Balliol scholarship, and that not only for the honour's sake—though the honour is the greatest part of it—but for the £30 per annum, which with an exhibition will, I trust, all but pay my way at Oxford, as Balliol is £20 or 30 cheaper than any other college.'

In November 1836 the Balliol scholarship was duly won. 'I have just come out from Balliol,' he wrote to his father on the twenty-sixth, 'of which College I am now a Scholar. The examination concluded this morning about twelve o'clock and it has just been given out. I have got Head one...' By this time it was no longer necessary for a letter home to plough its way for long months across the Atlantic. The Cloughs had returned to Liverpool in July and thenceforward, except for occasional business trips by James or his elder son Charley, were to remain at home. Anne, who was herself to develop into a woman of quite outstanding ability and achievement, always idolised her cleverest brother. She has a description of him as he appeared to her that summer, after five years of separation—a blooming youth of seventeen, with an abundance of dark soft hair, a fresh complexion, much colour, and shining eyes full of animation. About Arnold's influence over him the family were not so happy. 'This was,' Anne wrote long afterwards, 'his enthusiastic period, when, with the fervour of youth, he would pour out his soul. Dr Arnold was his hero, and it was striking to hear him expound his views. His father and mother were not quite pleased, the family being, by inheritance, Tory. They thought often perhaps he ought to have gone to Shrewsbury...'

Clough remained on at Rugby until the summer of 1837, mainly in order to try for the leaving exhibition—the final hurdle which this paragon of pupils, although he suffered from headaches and overwork after the triumph at Balliol, succeeded in clearing easily. By this time he had become beyond any question the prize colt in Arnold's racing stable, and in the January holidays of 1837 received the ultimate accolade of an invitation to spend ten days at Fox How, the house in the Lake District which the Doctor had built in consultation with Wordsworth. At the final prizegiving Arnold was moved to break the rule of silence concerning his pupils' achievements which he always observed on these occasions and publicly congratulated Clough on having gained every honour which Rugby could bestow, and in October, the month in which Clough took up residence at Balliol for the first time, he wrote to Clough's Uncle Alfred, a fellow of Jesus College, Oxford, in the following unqualified terms: 'I did not write to you when your nephew left us, but I must take the opportunity of one of our men's going to Oxford tomorrow, to send you these few lines. I cannot resist my desire of congratulating you most heartily on the delightful close of your nephew's long career at Rugby, where he has passed eight years without a fault, so far as the School is concerned, where he has gone on ripening gradually in all excellence intellectual and spiritual, and from whence he has now gone to Oxford, not only full of honours but carrying with him the respect and love of all whom he has left behind, and regarded by myself, I may truly say, with an affection and interest hardly less than I should feel for my own son.'

Eight years without a fault—it is a tremendous, almost unbelievable claim, especially coming, as it does, from one who, where the shortcomings of the human boy were concerned, was all-seeing and swift to pounce. Arnold's enthusiasm was understandable and just. Arnold was a man with educational theories, theories which were to carry great weight, and exert spectacular influence, not only on the England of his own day but also on the picked youth of succeeding generations of the English from his day to our own. In Clough he saw the triumphant vindication, the wholly successful human embodiment of these theories. No wonder he was pleased.

And yet, and yet—the paragon was, in the world's eyes at any rate, to disappoint. Even by the time of Arnold's early death in 1842 it was becoming clear that the prize pupil, the eager, impressionable clay, had finally turned his back on prizes, had begun already to turn moody and argumentative. In the sixties Arnold's greatest son, Matthew was to write a most moving, most melodious lamentation over Clough, was to call him Thyrsis, was to sigh over the 'too quick despairer' who had died untimely in the prime of life. W. G. Ward, reminiscing thirty years later about the Clough he remembered at Oxford, was to speak sadly of 'reaction', of 'his intellectual perplexity [which] preyed heavily upon his spirits'. Jowett was to speculate, concerning him, about the possibility of a defect of willpower. Even his sister, the adoring Anne, was to write to a friend a few weeks after his death lamenting 'the closing in of my most cherished hopes, which were born in the early dawn of my life, and which I have fed upon ever since. I have waited listening for him to speak, to utter thoughts that he had been pondering over during his life...'

What went wrong?

Before trying to answer that it is necessary to insist that nothing went wrong totally and irremediably. His is still a lonely, unique mid-nineteenth century voice. Much of what he wrote has quality enough to give it permanence. Bagehot, shrewdest of Victorian critics, praised him highly, and his praise can strike no present-day reader of Clough's work as misplaced. As we shall see he came before the end to acquire a sufficient measure of certainty to give his work poise and himself a sense of fulfilment. To the mature Clough—'with his hold on reality and his sympathetic modern accent', in Gosse's words—we can be grateful for much. We are not by any means reduced to thinking of him only as the best goalkeeper on record or as the most impeccable schoolboy ever to gladden the heart of a demanding headmaster.

All the same something did go wrong. Was it simply that the

glad, confident morning of October 1837 was altogether too bright to last, that some clouding over was only to be expected after such dazzling early brilliance? This would provide an easy, but quite unsatisfactory, explanation. Clough's talents were outstanding and they were genuine. It was simply not a case of a bright little schoolboy squib being outshone once fired into the larger, more competitive firmament of the university. Oxford was as impressed as Rugby. Frederick Temple, later Archbishop of Canterbury, wrote of the Oxford Clough in these terms: 'He seemed to me, when first I knew him, the ablest and greatest man I had ever come across, and the one from whom I had learned more than from any other man I knew.'

What was wrong was Dr Arnold, his engulfing personality and, paradoxically, that supreme schoolmasterly excellence which has, in many ways deservedly, reserved for him a place of honour in the sparsely populated pantheon of pedagogues. Arnold was of course an unconscious villain, a stimulating, gifted, beneficent villain whose wrongdoing was no more than over-zealous well-doing. The mess he made of Clough needs to be pointed at—in these days perhaps especially—with an insistent, threatening fore-finger. It highlights the unwisdom inherent in any attempt at a generalised theory of education; it calls attention to the un-doubted fact that any deviser of educational formulas, however reasonable, however well-documented, is likely to dig a deep, deep pit for himself the moment he ventures beyond the humble simplicity of What is good for Willy will be arsenic for Arthur. What Arnold achieved at Rugby undoubtedly had value. A system such as his, slavishly copied as it has been in hundreds of public schools up and down this country for the last century and a quarter —copied too, with some necessary modifications by the thousands of grammar schools which were the offspring of the Education Act of 1902—a system such as his must have supplied spectacularly effective answers to many problems. It did. The tough and turbu-lent barbarities which were the staple of English school life before Arnold's time—which were the accepted rule in, say, the Win-chester of his own boyhood or the Christ's Hospital of Leigh Hunt—became unpleasant, rather evil-smelling memories in the short space of a single decade simply through the force and dynamism of Arnold's example at Rugby. What Arnold offered satisfied Tom Hughes very well—and it satisfied, no doubt, all the thousands of other equable, outward-looking Tom Hugheses for whom an electrifying sermon in Rugby Chapel was no more than a quiet half hour with background solemn music useful for the digesting of too much pease pudding at luncheon.

But Clough wasn't a Tom Hughes; he was intense, and intelligent, as responsive as an Aeolian harp with all its strings stretched taut. Arnold's moral fervour, his insistence that it was a boy's duty to examine his conduct as minutely and as searchingly as his teacher examined his ability to conjugate the verbs in μι, turned Clough, not into the ordinary, lumpish, reasonably-behaved-for-once decent chap, but instead into the feverish, unnatural, guilt-ridden creature whom we watch writing those unctuous letters to Georgy in the Isle of Man. Arnold's insistence upon the importance of giving the young responsibility had not been formulated without much close and sympathetic observation. It proved wonderfully effective with the average, careless, negligent boy. Responsibility to such a one was like a cold shower, disagreeable and grumbled about in prospect, but bracing afterwards. On Clough, tenderly conscientious and with intelligence enough to see not only what obviously would have to be done for trouble to be avoided, but also what might be done if 'responsibility' were given its ultimate, Arnoldian sense, it became a nightmare and an incubus. 'Every sixth form Rugbeian'—so wrote F. H. Doyle in his *Reminiscences*—'was bound under Arnold's auspices to come of age in his teens and to wield the sceptre placed by the great headmaster in his hands, with solemn self-importance too apt to degenerate for a season into priggish self-importance.' This is too generalised. *Every* sixth form Rugbeian is much too sweeping. But it certainly points to a tendency which was observable in very many of Arnold's products, even if it can only be applied to Clough with reservations. Priggishness he did suffer from—how could the poor fellow help himself? But Clough could never be charged with self-importance. Excessive self-abandonment, a too fervent discipleship—it was in this quite contrary direction that he erred and strayed.

Must Arnold take the full blame for the disappointments which lay ahead for those like Temple—and there were very many like Temple—who were putting their money on Clough? Perhaps not the full blame. Perhaps for all his brilliance he was one of those who can never be truly happy unless he is being given a lead;

33

perhaps, for all the grasp and power and independence of his intellect, there was in him a basic, ineradicable need for the reassurance afforded by some strong figure, unhesitant and hot for certainties, to whom he could attach himself; perhaps, whatever training for manhood had been provided for him, the convolvulus strain would have remained and he would have put forth his flowers, beautiful, pale and starlike, only so long as there was a sturdy, positive tree trunk close at hand to cling to; perhaps, if no Arnold had been on hand to rally the young traveller as he marched 'on to the bound of the waste, on to the City of God', there would have had, inevitably, to be somebody else—as, later on, there were to be Ward perhaps, or Newman, or Florence Nightingale.

All the same there must have been many Cloughs, or near-Cloughs, on whom the effects of the Arnoldian system must have been, in some degree or another, deleterious. There have been many Cloughs, or near-Cloughs, in succeeding generations who have been warped and stunted by the evils of the system which Arnold's genius forged and perpetuated. It was, and is, a system which encourages and over-magnifies guilt-feelings which in the young and sensitive are almost always quite lively enough without any artificial boosting; it was, and is, a system which, by its too-frequent recourse to the easy and question-begging weapon of expulsion, tends to create an unhealthy hothouse atmosphere in a school. By the time the sixth form is reached the indigestible chaff has been winnowed out, the non-conformists have been shown the door, and there tends to remain an unnaturally high concentration of the imitative, the biddable, the over-enthusiastic and the time-serving; it was, and is, a system which, by its insistence on the paramount virtue of public-spiritedness and on the importance of always being up and doing, succeeds in suggesting that there must lie, in any timetable which makes provision for drifting and dreaming, something at once furtive and disreputable. Clough could have done with much more drifting and dreaming.

Finally the Arnoldian system was, and is, one which attempts to draw the frontier between Right and Wrong with an altogether impossible minuteness, exactness and definiteness. The unequivocal simplicities of the school-chapel sermon may well achieve their end of stimulating awareness in the young listener, but they may also invite a quite violent reaction once that young listener is out in the world and groping his way in places where everything is a dirty shade of grey and no brilliant, reassuring whites, no positive, forbidding blacks are anywhere to be seen.

Reaction. Perhaps that is the word which stays most insistently in the mind as one comes to the end of Clough's days at Rugby. Reaction, détente, swing-away—the king of schoolboys must himself have had forebodings of the kind of process which was now soon to begin. He wrote a poem for his *Rugby Magazine* and he called it 'The Longest Day'. The longest day is one of climax and brilliance, but this is not what the young gentleman dwells on. The longest day is also the herald of the long, slow degringolade towards the winter solstice when the tides of life ebb weakly away into the darkness.

> *Is it not awful then to think*
> *How growth and progress now are o'er?*
> *That we are on the mountain's brink,*
> *Where we have clomb to climb no more?*
> *And is it not a note of grief*
> *That each day now will be more brief?*
> *That strength of limb and might of mind*
> *Alike their limit here must find?*
> *Is there no echo of decay*
> *To temper thee, thou longest day?*

It is true of course that he goes on to console himself briskly in the Arnoldian manner with the thought that 'Goodness never fadeth/ And love's bright sun no winter shadeth', but the note of weariness, of youthful exhaustion brought on by over-work and over-stimulation, has nevertheless been sounded. 'We have clomb to climb no more'—so far as Clough was concerned that was a notion about himself that no one at Oxford would have entertained for a minute. It was, for all that, a notion that was to rankle in Clough's mind for over a decade.

35

Three

OXFORD welcomed him warmly and was prepared to be impressed. And outwardly he was indeed an impressive young man, with no hint of the inner weariness—perhaps even temporary exhaustion—showing. 'A most noble-looking youth' is one description from an Oxford contemporary. 'I never lost the impression of the beautiful eyes which I saw opposite me at dinner in Balliol Hall,' says another. And the stress is by no means solely on soulfulness and spirituality. He was lithe of limb and sizeable. He was tough, and not afraid of Spartan simplicity. His rooms in college were of the pokiest, and he passed a whole winter in them without a fire. He wanted to work, he used to explain, and these stern methods ensured long stretches of privacy as no visitor could stand the conditions for longer than a minute or two. He made no mention of another, perhaps equally relevant, fact: that the Cloughs were beginning to be hard up. Certainly the sternness with himself was no pose, no passing undergraduate fad which he was to outgrow after his first term or two. In his last year as an undergraduate, when he was living in lodgings off Holywell, he went into the Cherwell every morning throughout the winter. Tom ('Prawn') Arnold too was fascinated by his eyes and by 'the glorious flash' which would break from them after some sudden solution of a problem, and the 'fat fellow', Ward, his tutor at Balliol, 'was not so deeply attached to any of his Oxford friends as to Clough'.

Ward had been a tutor at Balliol for two years, since 1835, when Clough came up. Anne thought that Ward exercised a great influence over him, and indeed Clough himself once remarked to

Frederick Temple: 'When I am talking to Ward, I feel like a bit of paper blown up the chimney by a draught, and one doesn't always like being a bit of paper—so I sometimes keep away from the draught.' The strength of Ward's influence is less than once was thought—Clough kept away from the draught pretty effectively— but Ward remains none the less an important figure in Clough's life at this stage. He was his tutor for one thing, and therefore the most obvious recipient of the totally committed allegiance which the young man had till now been laying in the lap of Dr Arnold. Ward was also at the centre of the ferment and intellectual excitement which was agitating Oxford at this time and which had better be briefly looked at before going any further.

John Keble's sermon on 'national apostasy' was four years old when Clough went up to Oxford. It had been in July 1833, a week or two after the assize sermon, that a meeting had taken place at the rectory of the Reverend Hugh James Rose at Hadleigh in Suffolk. Those present at this meeting had been, apart from Rose himself, A. Perceval, William Palmer of Worcester College, and Hurrell Froude. Not present at the meeting, but firmly backing the extremist views of Froude and forming with him a ginger group, had been Keble himself and lastly, 'fresh from his escape from death in a foreign land, and from the long solitary musings in his Mediterranean orange-boat, full of joyful vigour and ready for enterprise and work', one man of towering genius, John Henry Newman.

What did these extremist views amount to? And what prompted the expression of them at that particular time? Parliament was proposing to appropriate part of the revenues of the Irish church and apply the money thus acquired (the figure of £60,000 was mentioned) to such purposes as it thought fit. In the event the idea of appropriation was abandoned, and all that happened was a merging of some bishoprics. Yet Keble, Newman, Froude and their friends were not to be deflected from the conviction that a critical time was at hand and high principles at stake. A secularised and liberalised church on the pattern of Whately or Arnold—'All societies of men, whether we call them states or churches, should make their bond to consist in a common object and a common practice, rather than in a common belief' was how Arnold put it— was anathema to them. Had belief in the apostolical succession gone out with the non-jurors? Then it was time that belief was revived. 'There was something greater than the Established Church,' wrote Newman, 'and that was the Church Catholic and Apostolic, set up from the beginning, of which she [the Church of England] was but the local presence and organ. She was nothing unless she was this. She must be dealt with strongly or she would be lost. There was need of a second Reformation.'

This Reformation was what was decided on at Hadleigh. The *Tracts for the Times*, beautifully written, as was to be expected with Newman as author-in-chief, began to be hawked around the parsonages, and, producing an effect more electrifying still, Newman began his famous four o'clock sermons in St Mary's. The university took all this with the greatest seriousness. In the thirties of the last century Oxford was of course a place far more closely connected with the established church than it is today. People in Oxford could talk of little else beside this new religious revivalism. You had to be for Newman or against him. It was felt there—though it is doubtful whether the country at large shared the feeling—that a grave crisis in the country's affairs was at hand. And when, in 1836, Melbourne appointed Hampden to the chair of divinity, Oxford grew more excited still. Hampden was an inconspicuous divine who thought along Arnoldian lines. The Newmanites thought he was shaky on the creeds, but Melbourne had not proceeded to the appointment without the concurrence of the Archbishop of Canterbury. It was difficult therefore for the Newmanites, proclaimed believers in apostolical succession and ecclesiastical authority, to attack the appointment openly. Instead they sniped at him meanly from behind convenient bushes, provoking Arnold, not far away in Rugby, to passionate fulminations. 'Formalizing, Judaizing fanatics,' he called them, 'who have ever been the peculiar disgrace of the Church of England.'

By 1837 Ward, impulsive, clever, tactless, unstable, had switched his allegiance from the Arnold-Whateleyites to the great Newman—'ὁ μέγας Νέανδρος' as Clough was calling him in 1838 in a letter to Gell. The whole situation was one which cannot have failed to have a considerably unsettling effect on Clough, however skilfully he tried to avoid being 'sucked up the chimney'. The large and corpulent Ward was assertive; he was also Clough's tutor, his mentor, and Clough was used to mentors if ever a young man was. And yet here was Ward writing to him from London in

38

July 1838: 'I had a long talk with Vaughan of Oriel last night who
...is perfectly certain...that Arnold and all Anglican *Protestants*
are in a false position...Arnold he thinks...understands neither the
grounds of the infidel nor of the Newmanist and will never give
himself the trouble to understand them...I was very glad to find
Vaughan apparently fully agreeing in my warm praise of [that
whole phase of] Newmanism...I do hope dearest that nothing may
happen to make me split from you decidedly in any opinion on
these matters: for you do understand me so much better than
anyone else that it would be a most serious mortification.'

So could 'the blessing of being under Arnold' have been a more
mixed blessing than Clough had thought? Might Arnold, the
confident seeker after truth, have gone rushing after it in the
wrong direction? If Arnold was wrong what sense could be made
of all his (Clough's) screwed-up, passionate endeavour over the
last years? What certainty about anything could there ever be if the
fountain of all certainty could be proved to have been spouting
nonsense all these years? No wonder Clough shrank away into the
background in an endeavour to avoid being singed by the fires of
religious controversy when the flames licked round in various
directions as Newman blew, or Ward blew, or Arnold blew. 'I do
not quite like,' he wrote to Gell at Cambridge in November 1838,
'hearing so much of these matters [theological, ecclesiastical,
political] as I do—but suppose if one can only keep steadily to
one's work, (which I wish I did) and quite resolve to forget all the
words one has heard, and to theorize only for amusement, there is
no harm in it.' He kept to this resolution and fended Ward off
somewhat brusquely, but Ward was at him again in a long letter
which he wrote to him on January 4, 1839, during the winter
vacation: 'I want you to take very great pains with your next letter,
to give the whole business a thorough thinking over from the
beginning of last Lent Term to the present time...' Writing long
years later when Clough was dead and his own head securely
pillowed on the bosom of the scarlet woman of Rome, Ward
admitted that he had been a meddler, that he had, where Clough
was concerned, given his passion for winning friends and in-
fluencing people too free a rein. 'What was before all things to
have been desired for him [Clough], was that during his undergraduate career he should have given himself up thoroughly to his
classical and mathematical studies, and kept himself from plunging

39

prematurely into the theological controversies then so rife at Oxford...After this premature forcing of Clough's mind there came a reaction.' Ward has certainly a lot to answer for where Clough is concerned. He caused Clough's idol to rock and totter drunkenly on his plinth before Clough was old enough to accept so awful a sight with equanimity, before he was old enough to accept resignedly the sad fact of universal human fallibility. Jowett wrote down his memories of Ward in the eighties, and although the Master strives for smoothness and benevolence, his claws are not wholly retracted. '[Ward] once took me on a Sunday evening, in the middle of summer, about the year 1839, when his change of opinions was still recent, to Mr Newman's church at Littlemore, where he was to preach...Two things I remember on that occasion which were highly characteristic of him. The sermon which he preached was a printed one of Dr Arnold's, but with additions and alterations which, as he said, it would have driven the author mad to hear...We walked back to Oxford in the twilight, along the Iffley Road. He was in high spirits, and sang to me songs out of *Don Giovanni*.' There can be no doubt that from Arnold to Ward was for Clough a rough, even perhaps a disastrous transition.

It may be doubted, though, whether Ward was right about the desirability of Clough's giving 'himself up thoroughly to his classical and mathematical studies'. What Clough found rather was that, on the academic side, Oxford had far to little to offer him. He had prepared himself too thoroughly, been crammed too full. He found, what over-prepared young open scholars to our older universities are finding too often even today, that instead of having to press on to a still distant winning post, they are required to slow down to a jogtrot, or even stop altogether and cast back towards the starting point.

He waited a long time before making public his views on the shortcomings of an Oxford education as he had experienced it. But when he was thirty-three he wrote a review of the Oxford University Commissioners' Report, published in 1852. He begins by setting out the strenuousness and extent—they are quite staggering —of his classical studies at Rugby. 'No words,' he goes on, 'can express the amount of the change which I experienced on entering the lecture-rooms of my college...Had I not read pretty nearly all the books?...I should have wished to take to mathematics...but mathematics alone would not lead to a Fellowship...What I wanted was to sit down to happy, unimpeded prosecution of some new subject or subjects...Surely there were other accomplishments to be mastered besides the composition of Iambics and Ciceronian prose. If there were, however, they existed not for me...The daily lectures now, and the weary re-examination in classics three years ahead! An infinite lassitude and impatience, which I saw reflected in the faces of others, quickly began to infect me...The masters of the public schools have, it is true, been at fault; they have pushed on their pupils too hastily...[but] surely, after the age of nineteen or twenty, it is really time that this schoolboy love of racing, this empty competition, should be checked...For the preliminary discipline of boys I grant it to be needful; to carry it forward into the very years of legal manhood appears to me...most foolish and ill-advised...Of all Senior Wranglers, Medallists, and even "Double First", let us be fairly and finally rid.'

Was this petulance? Did the fact that he had been the first Balliol scholar ever to take a second instead of a first in the schools still rankle in 1853? Did he still remember, as young Tom ('Prawn') Arnold remembered long years afterwards, his return to Rugby after the announcement of the results, his standing before Dr Arnold in the front court of School House, and his blank offering of the news 'with face partly flushed and partly pale: "I have failed" '? It is most unlikely. Clough's views on the Oxford curriculum have the ring of a considered and firmly held opinion. His own partial failure in the schools did not shake him at the time of its happening and did not betray him into emotional, ill-considered outbursts later. 'You must really not trouble yourself about my results,' he wrote to Anne in June 1841 shortly after their publication. 'I do not care a straw for it myself, and was much more glad to have it over than I was disappointed at hearing the result...it does not matter I think at all; and I can assure you it has not lessened my own opinion of my ability...if I got a 2nd with my little finger it would not have taken two hands to get a double first...neither must you think that it is about my class that I have been bothered during the last year, and that I *must* therefore be disappointed. I can assure you that it was principally about other things altogether, though you need not read or say this to Fath. and Mother.' Anne noted in her Journal: 'Was most exceedingly put out of the way last Sunday on hearing Arthur was only in the second class in the examination. I could not endure he should be beat by anyone.' His letter calmed her and she wrote comfortingly to him, and to this he replied a week later: 'I am glad my explanations have relieved your disappointment, though I hope you will not blab my bravado any further.' (This was the boast about what he could do with his little finger.) 'I am not sorry to lose reputation, for it is very often a troublesome companion.' Later in the month, after the visit to Rugby, Clough went home to Liverpool, and Anne noted: 'Arthur comes home...There has certainly been a quantity of show-off nonsense and attempt at talking finely about poetry etc., which A. did not seem to approve of, and put off. I want praise too much, yet he is the only person from whom I really desire it.'

But if Clough refused to be drawn as deeply into Tractarian controversies as his bouncy tutor supposed, and if, as he himself tells us, his second was got by the exercise of no more than his little finger, what was occupying him those three years? Poetry? There are a few pieces certainly that must be looked at, but not enough to occupy him for more than a very few weeks out of all that time. The lusts of the flesh? These must presumably have troubled him since there was nothing freakish or abnormal in his constitution. But there is no word, no hint of anything tangible in this line in any of his letters to his contemporaries, and Ward—not, of course, the most observant of men—affirmed that 'all—certainly all the tutors, and I believe all the undergraduates—greatly appreciated his singularly high principle and his exemplary spotlessness of life.' Lack of physical condition? He certainly began to lose much of his fine brown hair, but the unheated Balliol garret and the pre-breakfast winter plunges into the Cherwell point neither at genuine ill-health nor at hypochondria. Good works in the Arnoldian manner? Hardly, because he did not mingle with his fellows nearly enough for the dedicated do-gooder. Ward, indeed, became worried about his increasingly reclusive tendencies and tackled him about it. 'Every day he used to return to his solitary room immediately after dinner; and when I asked him the reason for this, he told me that his pecuniary circumstances incapacitated him from giving wine parties, and that therefore he did not like to wine with others.' Ward did not believe this altogether, and credited the young hermit with 'fastidiousness of taste and judgment...which prevented him from enjoying general society.'

Clough was primarily occupied with none of these things at this time. He was busy learning a different lesson. It was an elementary one, but nevertheless difficult to master when the learning had been postponed as late as it had been in his case. He was learning how to walk without leading strings. He had lived for seven years under Arnold's spotlights. He had lived in a perpetual glare where the shadows were knife-edged, where the whites were pure and spotless and dazzling and the blacks definite, loathsome and instantly recognisable. To pass from that to normal human daylight made him blink and grope. Could this new adult landscape really be so chaotic? Could the frontiers and the demarcation lines be so vague, the cross-roads so badly lit, the routes to salvation and to perdition run so bafflingly parallel to one another?

These were the questions which plagued him. The outward front which he maintained in his letters about this time is the common undergraduate one of flippancy. 'You must really come to Oxford,' he wrote to Gell on May 19, 1839. 'It is also advisable that you should see the Arch-Oxford-Tractator before you leave this part of the world, that you may not be ignorant on a topic doubtless interesting even to the remote barbarians in Van D's Ld.' [Van Diemen's Land, where Gell was going.] 'It is said that Romanists are increasing, Newmanists increasing, Socinians also, and Rationalists increasing perhaps, all other kinds of men rapidly decreasing; so that on your return to England perhaps you will find Newman Archbp. of Canterbury and father-confessor to the Queen; Lord Melbourne (if not burnt) excommunicated, and philosophers in the persons of the Apostles' apostolically ordained successors fairly and platonically established as Kings... You will also have the opportunity of seeing Conybeare Pater issuing fulminatory condemnations of the Fathers at the heads of astonished Newmanists from St Mary's pulpit: himself in shape, conformation and gestures most like one of his own icthyosauri and his voice evidently proceeding from lungs of a fossil character. Again you will see Chevalier Bunsen, Poet Wordsworth, and Astronomer Herschel metamorphosed into Doctors of Civil Law, a sight worthy, especially in the second case, of all contemplation. Furthermore there will be boat races with much shouting and beer-drinking, a psychological study of great interest.' It is all good, defensive, undergraduate stuff, very different from the rapt intensity of the letters to Georgy a year or two earlier. The public excitements and debates are talked about—he must appear to be in the swim—but clearly he has little patience with them, although they are concerned with religious matters and church matters which all his training, from those long private sessions with his mother in Charleston to the last pep-talk with Arnold at Rugby, has taught him to consider as of paramount importance. Why? Because they interfere with his efforts to establish an identity for himself. 'I only hope to escape the vortex of Philosophism and Discussion,' he wrote to Simpkinson in October of that year, '(whereof Ward is the centre), as it is the most exhausting exercise in the world.' And a month later, on November 25, he did escape for a brief while. He had to go to Braunston, near Rugby, to officiate as groomsman at his uncle's wedding. He wrote to Burbidge on the 30th: 'I got here (back to Oxford) last night at ½past ten after a terribly long walk of about 40 miles and nearly 20 of them in the dark. I walked in fact all but the whole distance from Dunchurch to Oxford, a very rash experiment, especially as the road is sufficiently ugly and the day was sufficiently rainy...I am tied to my room today by a strained ancle which I managed to get myself in feeling my way along the dark and dirty road. I believe part of my motive for attempting it was the desire to be as long out of Oxford as possible, and really notwithstanding the rain I enjoyed all but the last 10 miles exceedingly.' Clough, of course, was not the first, and certainly not the last, undergraduate, to fling away from the stifling familiarity of academic society in order to see if a long, lonely walk might help to quieten and resolve the tumults inside him. But he experienced the difficulties in an intenser form than most, first because of the quite exceptional strength of the influences he had to shake off and second because of the fineness and acuteness of his own perceptions. 'Good night again,' he wrote to Simpkinson on the last day of 1839, 'I would give much for the pleasant treadmill routine of school.'

The poetry he wrote at this time was, as has been said, minute in quantity. It is interesting and revealing, rather than magical. There is much failure of communication.

44

Come back again, old heart! Ah me!
  Methinks in those thy coward fears
There might, perchance, a courage be,
  That fails in these the manlier years;
Courage to let the courage sink,
Itself a coward base to think,
Rather than not for heavenly light
Wait on to show the truly right.

This is the last mystifying stanza of a piece later given the title 'The Higher Courage' which was written probably about the same time as the long walk from Dunchurch to Oxford. It is not mystifying so much because the poet's notions are subtle, elusive and profound as because he is not yet able to manage a very tight stanza form without allowing the rhymes to throttle the sense out of him. In it he is still hankering after the comfortable certainties of Arnold which he could accept without having consciously to will himself into acceptance. But the thing for him now in this bewildering, contradictory Oxford is not to will himself into the acceptance of any dogma forced on him from without, à la Pascal or à la Newman, but to recognise that the higher courage is the sort which tells him to withhold judgment even if the impression he gives by so doing is that of someone feebly indecisive. 'Here am I yet,' he says in another poem,

...Carrying on the child into the man,
Nothing into reality. Sails rent,
And rudder broken—reason impotent—
Affections all unfixed...

Coherence and certainty there must be somewhere—how else could Arnold march round his little empire with so unfaltering a tread? But they were elusive, and for the present he must be content to find them so.

Truth is a golden thread, seen here and there
In small bright specks upon the visible side
Of our strange being's particoloured web.
How rich the converse! 'Tis a vein of ore
Emerging now and then on Earth's rude breast,
But flowing full below. Like islands set
At distant intervals on Ocean's face,

45

We see it on our course; but in the depths
The mystic colonnade unbroken keeps
Its faithful way...

In one way he ought to have been better off at Oxford than he had been at Rugby. He had no longer to put up with the 'curse of being without a home'. Liverpool, and an admiring family now all returned from the American deep south, were always ready to welcome him in the vacations, but even here there was now little to bolster up any sense of security. Money was getting tight. The cheapest rooms in Balliol, the refusal to go to wine-parties because of his inability to give hospitality in return—these were not part of any undergraduate pose. There was an undercurrent of anxiety in the house at Liverpool. Cotton and James Butler Clough were no longer proving a lucrative partnership, and Clough began to spend much of his vacations away from home. The summer of 1839 and 1840 he was with Ward in the Lakes (it seems, strangely, to have been a case of the tutor's dependence on the pupil rather than the normal way round) and was home only for September. 'Even of Liverpool, however,' he wrote to Burbidge in October 1839, 'I got very nearly fond before the end of the vacation: the long stay at home was so exceedingly pleasant to me...I am afraid...there is great likelihood of my father's business breaking down before long.' The following summer he came home sooner and Anne noted in her journal for July: 'Get very much vexed about Arthur's not coming home; it seems unkind of him to stay so long away... Arthur came home in the evening. Saturday morning, getting ready and doing German with him. My displeasure evaporates.'

And so it all came down to his standing before Arnold and announcing to him, in that June 1841, 'I have failed.' 'Prawn' Arnold did not remember what his father's reply to this had been. Perhaps he made none. Dr Arnold was too outward-looking, too managing a man to have much intuitive, imaginative understanding of the mental states of others. Perhaps that look of puzzlement, which Strachey wishes on to him at all sorts of unlikely moments, did for once spread across his face on hearing this piece of news. No headmaster finds it easy to understand why one of his odds-on favourites should come in second. But there was something in the announcement which was more puzzling even than the sad fact of

46

comparative failure. And that was the tone in which it was made. Arnold, insensitive though he was in many ways, had been a schoolmaster much too long not to have been instantly aware of it. Clough was not apologetic; not self-reproachful, not cast-down, not even apparently, in any genuine sense, concerned. Clough was defiant.

Four

A FURTHER jolt, most unpleasant if not entirely unexpected, was to come in that summer of 1841. 'Since I wrote last,' he tells Gell on September 11, 'two important events have befallen me—first, my descent into a second class...and second, the failure of my father's commercial concern which took place while I was in Westmorland about a month ago.' Anne heard the news while staying with her aunt at Min-y-don near Colwyn Bay. 'Got a letter from mother which frightened me very much as to father's business. Father's letter arrives with news that all is up with him. I go home by coach—rather an amusing journey, saw a good many strange people. Find things very bad, father and mother very much out of spirits. The next week they began to mend. Arthur comes home and gets the promise of pupils.' The pupil question seems to have been the one uppermost in Clough's mind after his near miss in the examination. It was urgently necessary that he should begin to think of himself as a breadwinner. Would a second be enough to ensure him an adequate amount of teaching work? Arnold was immediately helpful. There was typhus fever at Rugby and Liverpool boys due to rejoin the school in September were in consequence kept at home. Clough, Arnold suggested, should take them on. Before he went back to Oxford he was able to leave his mother £90 of his earnings. 'It was...very profitable,' he told Gell, 'most of my Papas being rich.'

His purpose in going back to Oxford was to try for a fellowship at Balliol in November. He failed again, although Tait, then a Fellow of Balliol and later to be Archbishop of Canterbury, was strong in his favour. Letters are scarce during this black time for him. Anne was trying to get a school going, but so far without success. 'I must say I feel very desponding,' she wrote in her journal in December 1841. 'No prospect of any scholars, nor has George [his schooldays over] a situation. I have some notion of going out day governessing, if I can get leave. Arthur does not like this plan.' His father wrote him a Micawberish letter in February 1842: 'I think before [November] I can scarcely doubt that both George and I shall be in some way of earning wherewith to pay it ['It' was money advanced him by his brother Charles]. I do beg that you will not be injuring your health by over exertions and extra work of mind and body to accomplish that object [paying off the debt], as nothing on earth can compensate for *loss of health.*'

Less than two months later Clough, rallying well after this long run of misfortune and non-success, was elected to a Fellowship at Oriel, the central operations room of the Tractarian movement. Newman, though absent much at Littlemore, was a Fellow there and indeed was one of Clough's examiners for the Fellowship; Charles Marriott—'very silent, grave and almost sleepy'—a dedicated high churchman all his exemplary life through, was another member of the Common Room, as was also Church, later to become Dean of St Paul's and historian of the movement. 'At Easter,' Anne noted, 'Arthur came down from Oxford to see us, after he had gained the Oriel Fellowship. He was more like himself than he had been for a long time, talked more and seemed in better spirits.' Another thunderbolt was however shortly to be launched upon him, this time from Rugby.

George Cotton was a young man whom Arnold had appointed to his staff in 1836, a year before Clough's departure. He was another of the Doctor's bright stars, and Arnold thought most highly of him, though Wordsworth, who met the monocled youth, could not share this enthusiasm and bluntly said so—'a more unattractive youth (but he is not like a youth) I never saw'. Cotton decided he was in love with Jane, Arnold's eldest daughter, and Jane found him acceptable. The wedding was fixed for June 1842, but in May Cotton began to have doubts, and these quickly grew strong enough to make him break off the engagement. The effect on Jane was grievous, on her father indirectly fatal. He took first to his bed with a furious feverish attack, much as he had after Ward's tendentious visit long ago. He recovered from this and the attack left—the words are Stanley's in a letter he wrote to Clough

49

in June 1842—'no other traces than a most remarkable gentleness and quiet, of which I had seen the beginning in the extreme tenderness and kindness which he had shown to Cotton'. But on the evening of June 11 he suffered an attack of angina pectoris and died in the early hours of the following morning.

Clough was stunned. He went home to Liverpool for one day and seemed 'in great distress'. He went walking alone in the Welsh mountains. He had lost his leader. The onus of decision rested now upon his shoulders and upon his shoulders only. It was hard indeed to make any satisfactory sense of a world in which Arnold, a zealous furtherer of the divine purpose if ever there was one, could be struck down in the prime of life between bedtime and waking. Was it right for him to cling to his Fellowship when the mere fact of holding it constituted a continual and public affirmation of his adherence to the tenets of orthodox Christianity? His financial straits and the indecisiveness which all his life through he tended to prolong combined to persuade him that it was.

So he returned to Oxford in the autumn, worked doggedly away at his teaching, was in Liverpool at the end of September to say goodbye to his father and to his brother George who sailed for America on October 4, and in December was given a lectureship. Tait meanwhile had succeeded Arnold as headmaster of Rugby. Bonamy Price and Vaughan had both been thought of for the post, but Tait had been Clough's choice and he had indeed at the end of June written to the trustees expressing strong support of Tait's candidature. At Oxford he listened eagerly to reports of how the new broom was sweeping. 'He is said to flog more than Arnold did,' he told Gell in November, 'and to be very strict.'

Clough's own teaching was being much admired. He had a gift for it. He had pupils in Ireland in the summer of 1842 and never lacked for them at Oxford. His Rugby juniors were beginning to arrive at the university. Walrond, enormously conscientious and like himself a head boy at Rugby, came up at the end of 1842, and there were also the Doctor's own two sons Matthew and Thomas. Clough, still reclusive and ascetic in his habits as he had been as an undergraduate, depended on these three for what social relaxations he indulged in, and Walrond treasured the memory of Clough's strong influence all his days. 'My Oxford days,' he wrote, 'seem all coloured with the recollection of happy and most instructive walks and talks with him. We used to meet every day almost, though at different colleges; and it was my regular Sunday holiday to breakfast with him, and then take a long ramble over Cumnor Hurst or Bagley Wood.' Matthew Arnold remembered those Sunday walks too. 'Thyrsis', in which he sings his sweet-sad, melancholy farewell to Clough, is full of them.

> *And this rude Cumnor ground,*
> *Its fir-topped Hurst, its farms, its quiet fields,*
> *Here cam'st thou in thy jocund youthful time,*
> *Here was thine height of strength, thy golden prime!*

The midsummer vacation of 1843 was spent half with pupils at Grasmere and half in going abroad—the first of many European journeys which were to prove a valuable source of refreshment to him and which were to contribute materially to the quality of much of his best writing. He went with Walrond as far as Florence and Bologna, and Burbidge joined them at Leghorn. Clough had to leave for England before them in order to rejoin his Grasmere pupils. He crossed the Simplon, went up the Rhone and over the Grimsel Pass to Thun and Bern and thence home by Basel and the Rhine. He liked Switzerland much better than Italy because 'being continually lionised about galleries and the like' was 'far less agreeable than walking through the beauty of the country'. The Wordsworth influence, so plain in the Rugby poems, was still strong on him. Simpkinson saw him at Grasmere as he was returning home from a Scottish excursion; Stanley was at Fox How, hard at work on his life of Dr Arnold. Mrs Arnold, Clough noted, was 'very cheerful, more so a good deal than I expected to find her'. His moral scruples were still nagging at him. On October 8 he wrote to Gell: 'I do not think I am particularly inclined to become a Puseyite, though it is very possible that my Puseyitic position [as Fellow of Oriel] may be preventing my becoming anything else; and I am ruminating, in the hope of escaping these terrible alternatives, a precipitate flight from Oxford—that is, as soon as my Exhibition expires, for I cannot think of sacrificing £60 on any consideration. Also I have a very large amount of objection or rather repugnance to sign "ex animo" the Thirty-nine Articles [Arnold had had doubts on the same subject, doubts which had lasted from 1818 to 1828, the year of his appointment to Rugby] which it would be singular and unnatural not to do if I staid in Oxford, as without one's M.A. degree one of course stands quite still, and has no resource for employment except private pupils and private readings.'

In November came more bad news from Liverpool. Georgy, only just twenty-two, had been struck down by fever at Charleston and had died there after a very few days' illness, alone and far away from any members of his family although his father, outward bound from England, had got as far as Boston when the news reached him. Clough reached Liverpool by December 18 and did what he could to comfort the distressed womenfolk. 'Arthur's visit at home did me a world of good,' wrote Anne. He was 'very good in reading to us in an evening'.

Gell returned a brisk answer to Clough's doubts: 'Pray why not sign the XXXIX Articles? you must sign something, unless you mean to have nothing to do with anybody.' Perhaps this letter helped him a little over the hurdle; certainly the urgent need for him to inject some money into the wasting Clough economy was a strong persuader. His father was ailing. He came back from America in the summer of 1843 quite defeated. The little spark of fight left in him after the disaster of August 1841 had been utterly quenched by the news of Georgy's death, wholly unexpected, which had caught up with him at Boston. Soon it became evident that a physical decline, matching the broken spirit, had begun, and he died on October 19, 1844. By then Clough had signed, thereby ensuring that the smaller house they had moved into in Liverpool should not be wholly without support, or be dependent solely on Anne's gallant efforts to run a little school. 'I remember,' he wrote to Gell in July 1844, 'I was...in doubt about signing the Articles; I did however sign them, though reluctantly enough and I am not quite sure whether or not in a justifiable sense.' His personal affairs were not at this time kind towards long-drawn-out bouts of moral scrupulousness. The tone of his references to the Tractarian controversies became increasingly derisive. 'There is much report and really I believe some chance of Newman's going over to the Holy Mother at last,' he told Burbidge in October. And a month later, 'I saw Ward bye the bye yesterday.' (Ward was in hot water himself with the authorities over his book *The Ideal of a Christan Church*.) 'He appears to consider Newman in advance of himself towards the Eternal City—but from what he said, there does not appear to be any immediate prospect of an actual arrival there.' At the end of that month, however, there is a long letter to

Gell which attempts a more serious examination of his position. The signing of the Articles was by now ancient history and he had ceased to bother about it, he told him. He simply had faith in what was being done by his own generation, and was himself content to be an operative—'to dress intellectual leather, cut it out to pattern and stitch it and cobble it into boots and shoes for the benefit of the work which is being guided by wiser heads.' Fond as he was of Oxford it might be better for him to find himself a place at Stinkomalee (London University) amongst the irreligious because 'without the least denying Christianity, I feel little that I can call its power.' Whether the Spirit of the Age, whose lacquey or flunkey he submitted himself to be, would prove eventually to be an accepter, or a denier, of Christianity he couldn't in the least say, but he often wondered (recalling his journeyman metaphor) whether the Master he was working under wasn't carrying out his own operations elsewhere, and leaving him (Clough) to obey the directions of a bungler no better than himself. Gell could call all this, if he liked, the 'Lamentations of a Flunkey out of place', but certainly, he concluded, the 'Flunkey hath no intentions, of giving notice to quit at present.'

And so he stayed where he was. Teaching was something he could do and something he enjoyed doing. No pupils passed out of his hands profitless, and many owed him much. The hectoring, the feverish certainties, the Sinai-commandments which poor dead Georgy had had to endure from him when he had been at Rugby were all put aside. He was the least assertive of dons, most wary of enthusiasm and whole-hoggery, most tentative and hesitant in pointing out what he felt to be error. 'Several survivors,' wrote Walter Bagehot in 1862, 'may think they owe much to Mr Clough's quiet question, "Ah, then you think—?" ' He watched Ward, the lover of direct action and no compromise, busily scuppering the Oxford Movement by putting an extremist interpretation on the already sufficiently tendentious Tract Ninety, and finally going over to Rome in September 1845 with Oakely of the Margaret Street Chapel and Newman himself rapidly following. He became a member, indeed a highly regarded member, of the 'Decade', an exclusive debating society which, during its ten years of existence, from 1840 to 1850, played much the same role as the Apostles played over a far longer period at Cambridge. Many of the ablest minds of Clough's generation were members—Matthew Arnold,

Archbishop Tait, Jowett and Dean Church amongst others—and they all thought of Clough as making outstanding, even indeed the most outstanding, contributions to the discussions. His pronouncements were never of course extremist; never was there a more dedicated avoider of total commitment; but he was always listened to with the greatest interest and respect—especially for what he had to say on social and political questions.

Social and political questions indeed became very important for Clough in those years of his Oriel fellowship and remained a central preoccupation with him throughout his life. It would be wrong to think of him in these days as of some hard-pressed Laocoon endlessly wrestling with the serpentine prose of the Thirty-nine Articles. Ever since coming up to Oxford he can be said to have been busy clearing his mind of cant, but in the middle years of the 'forties the influence of Carlyle on him became stronger. This influence can be seen in the increased sensitiveness of his social conscience, and the blatant happenings in the great world outside Oxford—the Irish famine, the railway South Sea Bubble, blown bigger and bigger by the piratical George Hudson —gave particular point and aptness to what Carlyle was saying. The Carlylean influence is strong even in his own prose style. In 1847 he wrote a pamphlet called *A Consideration of Objections against the Retrenchment Association at Oxford during the Irish Famine*. It is a spirited performance. The luxurious living of the select Oxford few is chastised with vigour. 'Shall not we then, the affluent and indulgent' (he is willing to count himself among them though the household up in Liverpool is still a struggling one and the insurance money payable on the death of his father barely adequate), 'spare somewhat of our affluence, curtail somewhat of our indulgence that these...may have food while they work, and have work to gain them food?' 'Oh ye,' he apostrophises them in a fine Carlylean frenzy, 'born to be rich, or at least not born to be poor; ye young men of Oxford, who gallop your horses over Bullingdon, and ventilate your fopperies arm-in-arm up the High Street, abuse if you will to the full that other plea of the spirits and thoughtlessness of youth, but let me advise you to hesitate ere you venture the question, May I not do what I like with my own? ere you meddle with such edge-tools as the subject of property. Some one, I fear, might be found to look up your title-deeds, and to quote inconvenient scriptures.'

54

Anne was very close to him all through the years of the Oriel Fellowship. In May 1845 she, her mother, and Charles moved into a smaller house in Canterbury Street, Liverpool. Charles lived with them until February 1846 when he married his cousin Margaret and soon afterwards settled in Wales. Anne busied herself with her school until 1846, but then gave it up to devote herself to teaching in the National and Sunday schools. The coming of Arthur was the event she looked forward to above all others. And when he wasn't with her he sent her books and gave her advice. In June 1845 she went with him to the Lakes and met the Arnolds—'Matt very merry and facetious'—at Fox How, and she and Arthur talked about Baptism and Blanco White. In September he was with her again and there was more talk, again of Blanco White and also of the Atonement. In June 1846 she went abroad with him. They went through Belgium, thence through the Rhineland and into Switzerland to Como where they joined Charles and Margaret. He talked to her of future plans and of 'the necessity, or rather great benefit, of women finding work, and considering it a duty to do so, and also whether they are at liberty to choose their own paths in some cases (I mean single women), without reference to their families.' After the abandonment of her school, she still hankered after 'a more decided vocation of teaching' and he wrote to her in July 1847: 'I will consider the subject you speak of, my dear; on the whole I should incline to study arithmetic and grammar, *perhaps*—but you must remember that a great advantage is given by *any sort of cultivation* (Music, drawing, dancing!, German, French, etc., etc.) for intercourse with the poor. They feel this distinction very sensibly and carry their liking of a lady almost to the vice of liking a *fine* lady.' He was in Liverpool again early in October 1847 on his return from yet another reading party, this time at Drumnadrochet. 'Woe's me,' he wrote to Shairp on the third, 'but one doesn't like going back to Oxford nor coming to L'pool neither:—no, nor seeing the face of hat and coat-wearing man, nor even of elegantly attired woman.' But if Liverpool was distasteful to him after the wild splendours ot the Highlands, the delight which Anne took in his company must have gone most of the way towards consoling him. 'Arthur came home,' she noted in her journal. 'Arthur was very kind, in truth he is a sweet angel, so gentle and good and so considerate. He is the comfort and joy of my life; it is for him, and from him, that I am

55

incited to seek after all that is lovely and of good report...We had a pleasant, quiet talk on Sunday evening when he was at home. I told him of what M. and I had been talking, viz. eternal punishment, and that we did not like to believe it or think of it, and he said he had quite given it up, for the Greek words did not mean so much as that.'

'One doesn't like going back to Oxford'—by 1847 Clough was becoming increasingly dissatisfied with his job as Oxford tutor. The literal orthodoxies which, by the simple fact of holding his Fellowship he was tacitly subscribing to, were coming to sound more and more hollow. Things came to a head when, on December 18, 1847, Clough wrote to Hawkins, Provost of Oriel, in the following terms. 'I hope I am not troubling you with useless explanation, but a phrase new to me, which you incidentally used in conversation on Friday has remained upon my mind, and makes me think it wrong not to be a little more explicit with you. You spoke of a Tutor as a Teacher of the Thirty-nine Articles. For such an office I fear I can hardly consider myself qualified. I can only offer you the ordinary negative acquiescence of a layman...To a certain extent, I feel, decidedly, that my position is not consistent with tutorial functions, and with that feeling my desire to resign them is not unconnected.' For over a month the letters, polite but stiffish, passed to and fro between Hawkins and Clough, and by the end of January they both knew where they stood. Clough wrote to 'Prawn' Arnold from Oriel on the last day of January 1848: '...Meantime, in England we go on in our usual humdrum way. The ecclesiastical world agitated by all manner of foolish Hampden-rows: of the confused babble of which all quiet people are infinitely tired...I have asked Emerson to come to Oxford and received answer that he will...I have given our Provost notice of my intention to leave his service (as Tutor) at Easter. I feel greatly rejoiced to think that this is my last term of bondage in Egypt, though I shall, I suppose, quit the fleshpots for a wilderness, with small hope of manna, quails, or water from the rock. The Fellowship, however, lasts for a year after next June: and I don't think the Provost will meddle with my tenure of it, though I have let him know that I have wholly put aside adhesion to the Thirty-nine Articles.'

Emerson has his importance in Clough's story. Not separated by a generation, he was nevertheless sufficiently older than Clough—

sixteen years—for a close friendship between them to be unlikely, yet there were sympathies between them and certain parallelisms in their life stories. On September 9, 1832—when he was roughly the same age as Clough was in 1848—Emerson had preached a hair-raising sermon in the Second Unitarian Church of Boston, of which he was pastor. The rite of the Lord's Supper, he had told his congregation, was an empty formality; its daily re-enactment down the centuries was in accordance with no command of Jesus but just another bit of nonsense set going by St Paul. He had then written a letter of resignation to his parishioners and gone off to Hopkinton Spring, Massachusetts, to see what sort of allies the waters there would prove to be in his running fight with diarrhoea. This change in spiritual direction on Emerson's part caused no conscience-striken hesitancy such as can be detected in Clough's letters to Provost Hawkins of 1847–1848, yet for Emerson as for Clough it was a change calling for courage and bringing in its train material hazards.

This visit of 1848 was not Emerson's first to Europe. After a six months' trip which took in Malta, Sicily, Naples, Rome, Florence and Paris, he had landed at Tower Stairs on July 21, 1833, at seven in the morning and had walked up through the mostly unawakened city to lodgings he had been recommended to try at Mrs Fowler's in Punch Square. He had visited Coleridge in Highgate but had been disappointed. Prepared for conversation and enlightenment, Emerson had found himself engulfed in a monologue. 'The great man was sadly old and preoccupied' and 'not to be easily followed'.

At Craigenputtock with the 37-year-old Carlyle it had been different. Here in the two-storeyed stone house friendship was possible and good talk abounded. Emerson was able to note 'the comfort of meeting a man of genius'. The two men had recognised each other's quality just as much as they had been made aware of each other's differences. Emerson's tendency to float upwards into the clouds borne on visionary wings contrasted with Carlyle's earthiness.

Now, fifteen years older, Emerson was in England again—in England 'anchored at the side of Europe, and right in the heart of the modern world'. He was there to give lectures, invited by Mechanics' Institutes in Lancashire and Yorkshire, but stayed with the Carlyles in London before the tour began. He found

Carlyle changed. Physical ills—indigestion, insomnia—had made him bitter and increased his tendency to be autocratic and mistrustful of his fellow-humans. Young English intellectuals were finding him more and more unsatisfactory as a leader. As Froude wrote in his *Nemesis of Faith* published in 1849—the book which Sewell, Rector of Exeter, the college of which Froude was Fellow, burnt ceremonially before the undergraduates in Hall—'Carlyle! Carlyle only raises questions he cannot answer, and seems best contented if he can make the rest of us as discontented as himself.'

Young English intellectuals were in fact looking for a new leader, and considered that in Emerson they might well have found one. Clough's invitation of Emerson to Oxford, and his later frequent contacts with him in an exciting Paris, setting busily about its ablutionary task of getting rid of Louis Philippe, are proof of the strong interest, even hero-worship, which Emerson had succeeded in arousing. 'Everybody liked him,' Clough said, though Emerson himself had his reservations, if not about Clough then certainly about Oxford. It was a place, he thought, where 'you may hold what opinion you please so that you hold your tongue'. And he was of course made fully aware of the restlessness the place aroused in Clough and in many of his friends. 'Yet here young men,' Emerson wrote, 'thus happily placed, and paid to read, are impatient of their few checks, and many of them preparing to resign their Fellowships. They shuddered at the prospect of dying a Fellow, and they pointed out to me a paralytic old man, who was assisted into the hall.'

But there can be no doubt about the sincerity of Clough's discipleship. In Emerson he saw a man whose thinking was moving towards a radical re-shaping of society, whereas Carlyle's seemed now to be moving in precisely the opposite direction. Carlyle had no welcoming words for 1848, the year of revolutions. Emerson, in the thick of it in Paris, saw much there that he could approve of. He saw the ceremonies in honour of Concord, Peace and Labour held on May 21 after the *émente*, and the vast crowd in the Champ de Mars 'like an immense family the perfect good humour and fellowship is so habitual to them all'.

Later on in that memorable year, in July, Emerson embarked again for home from Liverpool. Clough was there to see him off, and paid his parting tribute: 'What shall we do without you? Think where we are. Carlyle has led us all out into the desert, and he has left us there.' For Clough, shoulderer of burdens, Emerson's reply to this must have had a familiar, if none the less inspiring, ring. 'Clough, I consecrate you Bishop of all England. It shall be your part to go up and down through the desert to find out these wanderers and to lead them into the Promised Land!'

Did Clough by this time think of himself as a writer, as a poet? If he did it was with no very great measure of confidence. The idea of supporting himself by his pen struck him as wild and risky. He had too little readiness, too little flexibility to write gainfully for the periodical press. The number of publications for which he might conceivably write was severely limited by his own enormous conscientiousness. A paper had to have principles before Clough could write for it—principles with which he could find himself in close agreement. Apart from the pamphlet on retrenchment at Oxford—vigorous in its Carlylean way, if somewhat blunted in its impact because of Clough's obsessive awareness of the fact that there is always much to be said on both sides of a question—there was little he could point to in the way of printed-and-published prose accomplishment. Nor was poetry exactly gushing from him. At the end of 1847 he and Burbidge pooled their poetic capital and began submitting it to publishers. This was the volume later called *Ambarvalia*, which contains the bulk of what poetry Clough wrote during his time as Fellow and Tutor of Oriel.

Ambarvalia was not published until January 1849, when the volume appeared—slim, sombre-grey, a bit exercise-book-looking, under the imprints of Chapman and Hall, London, and Francis Macpherson, Oxford. Clough's contribution made up the first sixty-four pages of the book, and the rest was Burbidge's.

Why did he team himself up with Burbidge—a man whose poetical stature was never more than knee-high? The answer to this throws light on two important strains in his complicated character. He had an innate, abiding and total humility. And, out of all the gifted men who lived their lives in his thrustful century he was the very last one to whom the term 'careerist' could be applied.

The book received small attention from the critics. The *Guardian* however noticed it on March 28, 1849. Its critic's comments on Clough's share contained a roughly even mixture of praise and blame. Burbidge got a thorough and not undeserved dressing-down. Clough's forty poems were reissued separately in

1850, but only twenty-four of them were reprinted in the first posthumous collected edition of 1862. A complete re-print had to wait until Milford's *Poems of Clough* of 1910.

One of the best, and most revealing, of them is 'The New Sinai'. It is about man's restless, compulsive quest for God down the ages:

> As men at dead of night awaked
>   With cries, 'The king is here',
> Rush forth and greet whome'er they meet,
>   Whoe'er shall first appear;
> And still repeat, to all the street,
>   ''Tis he—the king is here;'
> The long procession moveth on,
>   Each nobler form they see,
> With changeful suit they still salute
>   And cry, ''Tis he, 'tis he!'

The pronouncement on Sinai comes to put an apparently final full-stop to all this:

> ...On Sinai's top
> Far seen the lightnings shone,
> The thunder broke, a trumpet spoke,
> And God said, 'I am one.'

But

> God spake it out, 'I, God, am One;'
>   The unheeding ages ran,
> And baby-thoughts again, again,
>   Have dogged the growing man:
> And as of old from Sinai's top
>   God said that God is One,
> By Science strict so speaks he now
>   To tell us, There is None!
> Earth goes by chemic forces; Heaven's
>   A Mecanique Celeste!
> And heart and mind of human kind
>   A watch-work as the rest!

What is the baffled mid-nineteenth-century thoughtful man to do in the face of all these competing claims? Reject the lot as cancel-

60

ling each other out, and, looking determinedly neither before nor after, pluck the flowers or nettles which each day brings? No, Clough is still the best head boy Arnold ever had. Heedlessness and irresponsibility can never, in any circumstances, be right.

> *Take better part, with manlier heart,*
>   *Thine adult spirit can;*
> *No God, no Truth, receive it ne'er—*
>   *Believe it ne'er—O Man!*
> *But turn not then to seek again*
>   *What first the ill began;*
> *No, God it saith; ah, wait in faith*
>   *God's self-completing plan;*
> *Receive it not, but leave it not,*
>   *And wait it out, O Man!*

And how movingly again in '*Qui Laborat, Orat*', he epitomises this, the central predicament of his generation:

> *O not unowned, thou shalt unnamed forgive,*
>   *In worldly walks the prayerless heart prepare;*
> *And if in work its life it seem to live,*
>   *Shalt make that work be prayer.*

He wrote well about friendship too and about how the trust and stress of competing ideologies and religious sytems could set friends on different courses and leave them, if not estranged, at any rate talking only faintly to one another across unbridgeable distances. '*Qua Cursum Ventus*' must be taken as a memorial to his friendship with Ward, and it is wholly successful. The sea comes into it, the sea and the white-topped ships he remembered riding at anchor alongside the wharves at Charleston.

> *As ships, becalmed at eve, that lay*
>   *With canvas drooping, side by side,*
> *Two towers of sail at dawn of day*
>   *Are scarce long leagues apart descried...*
> *E'en so—but why the tale reveal*
>   *Of those, whom year by year unchanged,*
> *Brief absence joined anew to feel,*
>   *Astounded, soul from soul estranged?...*
> *But O blithe breeze; and O great seas,*

Though ne'er, that earliest parting past,
On your wide plain they join again,
Together lead them home at last.
One port, methought, alike they sought,
One purpose hold where'er they fare,—
O bounding breeze, O rushing seas!
At last, at last, unite them there!

And there were the poems—precursors of a much finer one shortly to come—which came to him during those summer reading parties either in the Lakes or in the Highlands of Scotland. In one or two of them there is a hint, no more than a hint, that for Clough as for other men the sexual life was also a life that had to be lived. It is extremely difficult to be certain how intense a preoccupation this was for him. The curtains of reticence come down; they are made of impermeable stuff and there is never a gap in them. To all outward appearance it is a sexless world, monkish, freakish almost, this world of the Oxford senior common rooms of the early 1840s. The poems Clough wrote at this time which come nearest to the matter are the two called 'Love, Not Duty' and 'Love and Reason'. He makes it clear that he thinks love should be allowed to frisk and kick up its heels despite any disapproving frowns from those two stern taskmasters duty and reason. Are the swift, passionate certainties of earthly love, wholly impatient of any slow balancing of moral pro and con, the things that really matter?

I cannot say—the things are good:
Bread is it, if not angels' food;
But Love? Alas! I cannot say;
A glory on the vision lay;
A light of more than mortal day
About it played, upon it rested;
It did not, faltering and weak,
Beg reason on its side to speak:
Itself was Reason, or, if not,
Such substitute as is, I wot,
Of seraph-kind, the loftier lot.

Clearly so far as Clough was concerned the heart had to be allowed its reasons, but there is for all that something academic and un-lived about his treatment of the theme. He comes nearer to the realities of personal experience in his poem of farewell to the Highland Lassie. *My* Highland Lassie he calls her and says that he will

> *...call to mind the day*
> *The day that's gone for ever, and the glen that's far away;*
> *I shall mind me, be it Rhine or Rhone, Italian land or France,*
> *Of the laughings and the whispers, of the pipings and the dance;*
> *I shall see thy soft brown eyes dilate to wakening woman thought,*
> *And whiter still the white cheek grow to which the blush was*
>   *brought...*

And the sudden unspoken surge of mutual attraction when the young woman sits down beside him in the second class car is noted in '*Natura Naturans*':

> *In me and her—sensation strange!*
>   *The lily grew to pendent head,*
> *To vernal airs the mossy bank*
>   *Its sheeny primrose spangles spread,*
> *In roof o'er roof of shade sunproof*
>   *Did cedar strong itself outclimb,*
> *And altitude of aloe proud*
>   *Aspire in floreal crown sublime;*
> *Flashed flickering forth fantastic flies,*
>   *Big bees their burly bodies swung,*
> *Rooks roused with civic din the elms,*
>   *And lark its wild reveillez rung;*
> *In Libyan dell the light gazelle,*
>   *The leopard lithe in Indian glade,*
> *And dolphin brightening tropic seas,*
>   *In us were living, leapt and played...*

Mrs Clough found the poem 'abhorrent'—she was a woman easily horrified, and her husband's writing produced this effect on her frequently—and fought to have it omitted from the 1862 edition. 'The only thing I particularly desire to leave out is "*Natura Naturans*" which is abhorrent to me.' And in the same letter to Norton she says: 'I do know that, at least in this country, it is liable to great misconception.' Perhaps it is as well that she didn't write to Emerson in this vein, because there are strong Emersonian echoes in the poem. There can be seen in it too some

63

quite extraordinary anticipations of D. H. Lawrence's way of looking at the sexual situation.

But for all these occasional curvetings of the natural man the weight of the evidence in Clough's early poems is for repression and decorum. Conduct for him is still three-fourths of life. Duty, discipline, obedience—these are the abstractions which man must inscribe on his banner if he is to reach earthly fulfilment. Do thou the law, in fact, and thou shalt know the doctrine. Or, as he put it in

> *The Summum Pulchrum rests in heaven above;*
> *Do thou, as best thou may'st, thy duty do:*
> *Amid the things allowed thee live and love;*
> *Some day thou shalt it view.*

Only occasionally, towards the end of his Oxford years, when the decision to give up Fellowship as well as Tutorship was hardening— perhaps the crucial decision of a life which made almost a duty of indecisiveness—does a sudden savage impatience at his own too ready submissiveness and at the limitless hypocrisy of the world he saw about him overwhelm his restraint and give his verse tang and satiric bite:

> *Duty—'tis to take on trust*
> *What things are good, and right, and just...*
> *Stunt sturdy limbs that Nature gave,*
> *And be drawn in a Bath chair along to the grave.*

And there is 'The Latest Decalogue' which is terse and brilliant, highlights humanity's readiness to do the right things for the wrong reason as cruelly as anywhere in literature, and shows that there was always a La Rochefoucauld sleeping a dormouse sleep somewhere inside Clough but ready, at rare intervals to rub his eyes, speak up and startle.

> *Thou shalt have one God only; who*
> *Would be at the expense of two?*
> *No graven images may be*
> *Worshipped except the currency:*
> *Swear not at all; for, for thy curse*
> *Thine enemy is none the worse:*
> *At church on Sunday to attend*
> *Will serve to keep the world thy friend:*

Arthur Hugh Clough

The principal church in Charleston, South Carolina

Big school at Rugby

Oriel College

Two influences: Thomas Arnold and Florence Nightingale

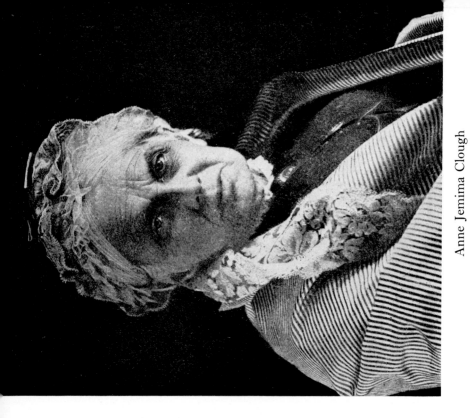

Anne Jemima Clough

W. G. Ward

J. A. Froude

Matthew Arnold

Ralph Waldo Emerson

Honour thy parents; that is, all
From whom advancement may befall;
Thou shalt not kill; but need'st not strive
Officiously to keep alive:
Do not adultery commit;
Advantage rarely comes of it:
Thou shalt not steal; an empty feat,
When it's so lucrative to cheat:
Bear not false witness; let the lie
Have time on its own wings to fly:
Thou shalt not covet, but tradition
Approvals all forms of competition.

He went back to Oriel at the end of January 1848, with one more term of tutoring to do and rejoicing to see before him the end of his servitude. He left an anxious household behind him in Liverpool. His mother was distressed, could not understand him, thought him ridiculous, and he had not the courage to tell her that he was abandoning a position of consequence and a tolerable salary because he had religious doubts. Some more of what he called 'unsavoury adaptations of scripture' in the manner of the 'Decalogue' appear in a letter he wrote to Anne on April 18: 'Tell Mother not to finish *all* her furnishing and "get everything handsome about her" before I come home. I don't think I shall do so, however, before Easter; but after; i.e. about the 1st of May, for then I shall be able to stay on if I please for three weeks or more, as my Tutorship will be in the hands of another; Matthias being ready to succeed, Judas will be free to go and hang himself.' Suddenly however the intention to return home was altered.

Instead he decided to give himself a holiday and went to Paris. For him this was, in effect, his final leavetaking of Oxford. His Fellowship was his, if he wanted it, until June 1849, and from the material point of view he wanted it badly enough. He had entered into an arrangement with one of the Clough family which bound him to pay an annuity of £100 in return for his right to the reversion of the capital on death; it was a time of low investment yield so that his mother's means were as scanty as they were ever likely to be. But these harsh facts were not strong enough to persuade him into thinking up excuses for holding on to the emoluments of the Fellowship whilst rejecting the more overt

65

commitment of being a tutor. Clough was always too honest a man for casuistry. His formal resignation of the Fellowship did not come until October, but from May until then he was only fleetingly in Oxford. Matthew Arnold, in the lovely yet misleading poem he wrote round him after he was dead, called back to life the incomparable Oxford they had known together. 'Too quick despairer' he called him:

> *Too quick despairer, wherefore wilt thou go?*
> *Soon will the high Midsummer pomps come on,*
> *Soon will the musk carnations break and swell,*
> *Soon shall we have gold-dusted snapdragon,*
> *Sweet-William with his homely cottage-smell,*
> *And stocks in fragrant blow;*
> *Roses that down the alleys shine afar,*
> *And open, jasmine-muffled lattices,*
> *And groups under the dreaming garden-trees,*
> *And the full moon, and the white evening-star.*

He hearkens not!...

No. He hearkened not. Firm and unchangeable, not to be shirked or sidestepped or postponed for further consideration, one fact stood fast amid the ebb and flow of thoughts and second-thoughts: he could not stay where he was. 'Another three weeks,' he told Shairp on March 16, 'will see me at the end of these tutorial—what shall I call them?—wearinesses, now at any rate. But whither the emancipated spirit will wing its flight, can't be guessed, Paradise, or purgatory or—? The limbo of meditation, the penal worms of Ennui, or the paradise of—?

VANITAS VANITATUM
OMNIA VANITAS'

Five

CLOUGH reached Paris on May 1, 1848. Did he think of Caesar and his Rubicon as the boat bore him towards the French coast? It is most unlikely. His willed change of circumstances was still far too negative, far too hesitant to justify any brisk soldierly analogies. Certainly he was taking a risk. He knew enough about himself to know that he was not the sort of person to whom the making of money comes effortlessly like breathing. Before there could be a prospect of his making even a tolerable living out of writing there would have to be a substantial increase in his capacity for fluency. Drastically and deliberately he had just imposed a severe handicap upon the exercise of his undoubted gifts as a university teacher. There was the chance, presumably, of something suitable turning up in Stinkomalee, and apart from that there was nothing much in the teaching line for him to hope for.

Was he justified in cutting himself off from the place where he was likeliest to do his most effective work? Was Matthew Arnold's phrase, 'too quick despairer', the right one for him? What wrong would there have been in his imitating the brisk insouciance which Thomas Arnold had shown in 1828, when he had signed his adherence to the Thirty-nine Articles because by doing so he was furthering the work which he felt himself in this world best able to accomplish? 'A common practice, rather than a common belief'—wasn't that what Arnold had said, and did not he (Clough) find himself after all in entire sympathy with the Christian code of ethics? These are questions to which a variety of answers has been found. J. I. Osborne, writing in 1920, thought that his personal relations had much to do with it. Matthew Arnold had given up

67

his Fellowship in 1847 in order to become private secretary to Lord Lansdowne, Lord President of the Council, and it was certainly to him rather than to Ward that Clough, especially as writer and poet, felt the closest attraction in the last years of his time at Oxford. It was Matthew who wrote to him in December 1847, putting his finger on what was undoubtedly in his eyes the central weakness of Clough's poetry up to that time:' a growing sense of the deficiency of the *beautiful* in your poems, and of this alone being properly *poetical* as distinguished from rhetorical, devotional or metaphysical, made me speak as I did.' Osborne thought too that Clough's restlessness and sudden brusque abandonment of his career might well be put down to purely physical causes. The 'singularly high principle and his exemplary spotlessness of life' which Ward praised in Clough the undergraduate had been carried faithfully forward into his time as Tutor and Fellow. He had remained celibate, and there is not the slightest hint, either in his own writings or in others', that he had not also remained a virgin. (It is true, of course, that the iron curtain which Victorian males succeeded in rigging up round their sexual lives is the most totally impenetrable contraption ever devised by a sex which in no age of history has been lacking in subterfuge in this matter; but the whole tone of the poems he wrote up to the late 'forties leads one to suppose that his sexual experience, if not entirely non-existent, was certainly minimal.) There are plentiful hints, on the other hand, that a celibate life was not the life of his choice. He may not have wanted to marry at the end of 1847 but he certainly wanted a woman. Miss Woodward, a more recent student of Clough, puts his resignation down in the main to his conscience. And certain it is that Clough's conscience was the tenderest, most unsleeping thing in all his complicated make-up. 'Conscience, then', says Miss Woodward, 'made a twofold revolt: against continued acceptance of a false intellectual position and against continued inhalation of a corrupt moral atmosphere.' There can be no doubt that the pamphlet on *Retrenchment at Oxford* provides solid proof that Clough's mind was much exercised at this time with the question of privilege on the one hand and piteous lack of it on the other. He was beginning to live up to the superscription of the letter which Matthew Arnold jokingly addressed to him at Oriel: 'Citizen Clough, Oriel Lyceum, Oxford.' It is not so

68

certain that the 'falseness of his intellectual position' was any more of a burden in 1847 than it had been at the time of his election at Oriel in 1842. And those frequent meetings with Emerson in the spring of 1848 may have sharpened his discernment of a basic—and deplorable—conventionality in his tacit acceptance of things which his mind told him he had no business to accept.

Yet these explorations of Clough's motives on the part of two discerning writers—shrewd and well-documented though they are—fail wholly to convince because they do not go back far enough. Clough's malaise has its roots and *raison d'être* not so much in Ward or in Newman or in 'The Two Nations' or in any highland lassies, real or imaginary. It springs from Thomas Arnold and the Rugby he created—the Rugby which staked out with bold unhesitant strokes the frontiers between vice and virtue, which set up stern fingerposts pointing along the narrow undeviating paths of duty towards ultimate Truth, which hummed with zeal and was briskly impatient of waywardness, dawdling, and second thoughts, which brimmed with confidence under the leadership of a man who thought of himself as one of the servants of God—'or sons', as Matthew Arnold was to write later in 'Rugby Chapel',

> *Shall I not call you? because*
> *Not as servants ye knew*
> *Your Father's innermost mind.*

For Clough, gifted, intelligent, biddable, the Rugby treatment was all wrong. For him who, paradoxically, dearly loved and was too readily responsive to, a strong lead in spite of his own outstanding qualities of judgment and perceptiveness, Arnold's dynamism was as dangerous as a finger of whisky to a pathological alcoholic. What he needed at school was to be left alone, to be allowed to drift, to come to himself slowly and sedately so as not to outrage that indolence and diffidence which he inherited from Anne Perfect and which were fundamental to him. He reached Oxford exhausted and bewildered. He was a forced plant which had produced a dazzling show-crop after seven years in a hothouse. Once transplanted into natural soil and natural temperatures he wilted. It took him ten years to achieve any sort of adaptation. It took him ten years to achieve even some sort of provisional understanding of the sort of person he really was. His break with Oxford can be best thought of as a kind of flourish of trumpets to announce that he was Clough and not Arnold's prize pupil any more, that biddableness and indolence and intelligence and creativeness and conscientiousness and lust were all part of him, and that before he could begin to work out any formula or way of life which would allow all these warring parts of him to co-exist harmoniously he must turn his back on a career chosen for him by others. He must symbolically walk out of his prison-house and slam the doors behind him. And what if this career chosen for him was the one he was really best suited to? What if he had to admit to himself that he liked it well enough? What if money was going to be tight and a job hard to find? Relevant questions certainly, but not ones which at that point of his development he was disposed to find answers to. Before all else he must be his own man.

So he went to Paris. 'Living in this state of suppressed volcanic action', as he described it in a letter to Anne on April 18, was over. He had erupted. Emerson was in Paris too. They dined daily together, were there for five weeks and together watched the struggle for power between the middle class and the workers which followed upon the revolution of the days of February. (Clough had a knack of making his visits abroad coincide with periods of civil tumult. He was to get several whiffs of grapeshot later on in Rome.) The elections of April 23 made it look as though France, freed now of the July monarchy and Louis Philippe, the little fat man with the green umbrella, was going to rally behind the middle class. Lamartine, speaking harmoniously and at length on all possible occasions, noted with satisfaction that 'the democrats prevailed over both the reactionary and the demagogic. 'But Paris, standing then as now well to the left of the country as a whole was dissatisfied with the way in which the elections had gone. On May 15, led by those experts in mob violence Barbès and Blanqui, the workers broke into the Palais Bourbon, sent the legally elected Assembly packing, and formed a government of socialists with Louis Blanc and Barbès as leaders. The Government however reacted strongly; the National Guard was called out and Barbès was arrested at the Hotel de Ville. 'Ichabod, Ichabod,' writes Clough excitedly to Stanley on May 19, 'the glory is departed! Liberty-Equality and Fraternity, driven back by shopkeeping bayonets, hides her red cap in dingiest St Antoine. Well-to-do-ism shakes her Egyptian scourge to the tune of "Ye are idle, ye are idle"; the tale of bricks will be doubled: and Moses and Aaron of Socialism can at the best only pray for plagues; which perhaps will come, paving-stones for vivats, and *émeutes* in all their quarters.' 'Meantime,' he goes on, 'the glory and the freshness of the dream is departed.'

His letters at this time—graphic, high-spirited, zestful, some of the best he ever wrote—are full of the struggle in France which prolonged itself into the beginning of June. Clough was back in England by June 6, and wrote on that day, from Long's Hotel in Bond Street, again to Stanley: 'I am safe again under the umbrageous blessing of constitutional monarchy...I left Paris yesterday. The *République* was "as well as can be expected". ' The uncertainty of Clough's 'as well as can be expected' was borne out in the next week or two. The Palais Bourbon government deliberately engineered a show-down with the socialists by closing the *ateliers*, or national workshops. The workers mustered threateningly in protest but Cavaignac, the war minister, given *carte blanche* to deal with the situation and backed by an adequately nourished National Guard, defeated them after a four-days' blood bath. The Second Republic was as good as done for, and the slogan '*Mais voulez-vous du bon? Choisissez Napoléon*' began to be heard in the streets. Clough, reviewing the exciting weeks in a letter to Tom Arnold on July 16, wrote: 'After the 15th [May] the sky was certainly overcast, but in my first fortnight, and in a degree throughout the whole time, I was in extreme enjoyment, walked about Jerusalem and told the towers thereof with wonderful delight; the great impression being that one was rid of all vain pretences, and saw visibly the real nation...The four days of June I dare say you have heard spoken of in a somewhat shrieky accent ...However, there is no doubt that France's prospects are dubious and dismal enough.'

Was it all simply an exiting raree show for him, or were his sympathies genuinely engaged? If such a question had been put to him that summer he would probably have had difficulty in providing an honest answer. A qualified, ring-side radicalism had been apparent in the Oxford Retrenchment pamphlet; the daily talk with Emerson must have strengthened his conviction that the future lay with the left. 'The wildest and most écervelé republican going' was how he described himself, and if there is self-mockery here there is an obstinate substratum of glowing pride as well. But undoubtedly some of the republican verve of his letters comes from his seeing, in the Paris events of May 1848, a sort of personal symbolism. He thought he saw a people rousing itself from sloth and servitude, and, swooping from the general to the particular, what was Arthur Hugh Clough doing if not precisely that? 'He rejoiced in his freedom,' Anne wrote. 'And for a time gave up all thoughts of the future.'

After Paris he went to Patterdale, where Fisher, a fellow don, was conducting his first reading-party. From there he returned to Liverpool, and, composing hexameters in English at the incredibly swift rate of some seventy or so a day, finished *The Bothie of Tober-na-Vuolich: a Long-Vacation Pastoral*, in one month. In the biographical chronology he wrote for his wife, he says: 'Wrote "the bothie" at L'p'l in September.' Anne says that he wrote it in October. He read aloud to her and her mother, she says, 'Longfellow's poem of "Evangeline", and almost immediately after began "The Bothie".' He wrote it in the upper room of the small house in Vine Street which looked out over some open ground, in those days unbuilt upon, just below Edge Hill. There were unfinished houses to see, and vacant building lots, and the spewed-up chaos produced by the railway-builders. He would rush out very early in the morning for some exercise before setting to work, and all that he saw on those dawn-constitutionals is crammed into one breathless, vivid Homeric simile which occurs towards the end of the poem:

> But as the light of day enters some populous city,
> Shaming away, ere it come, by the chilly day-streak signal
> High and low, the misusers of night, shaming out the gas-lamps—
> All the great empty streets are flooded with broadening clearness,
> Which, withal, by inscrutable simultaneous access
> Permeates far and pierces to the very cellars lying in
> Narrow high back-lane, and court, and alley of alleys:
> He that goes forth to his walks, while speeding to the suburb,
> Sees sights only peaceful and pure…

Then his tracking camera-eye flits over a number of exactly
caught pictures, finishing with the

> *Little child bringing breakfast to father that sits on the timber*
> *There by the scaffolding; see, she waits for the can beside him;*
> *Meantime above purer air untarnished of new-lit fires:*
> *So that the whole great wicked artificial civilised fabric—*
> *All its unfinished houses, lots for sale, and railway out-works—*
> *Seems reaccepted, resumed to Primal Nature and Beauty.*

It is Wordsworth's Sonnet on Westminster Bridge forty years on.
Less ruminative, less sculpturally sonorous, more break-neck, it
can stand comparison with it. It is no better, and no worse, than
dozens of other passages scattered up and down this breathless,
exhilarating poem. He wrote, Anne said, 'in a ferment and excitement, but enjoying and rejoicing in his work.' 'This genius of
Clough,' Emerson noted in his Journal in December 1848, 'how
excellent, yet how slow to show itself…now I have a new friend,
and the world has a new poet.'

The Bothie is about young men wanting to be in love. There is a
story. A group of undergraduates are gathered in the Highlands to
do some reading with their tutor—'the grave man, nicknamed
Adam'. They attend a gathering of the clans at the estate of the
Chief, Sir Hector, and there Philip, one of Adam's party, is
invited by 'a thin man clad as the Saxon' in these terms:

> *Young man, if ye pass through the Braes o'Lochaber*
> *See by the lochside ye come to the Bothie of Tober-na-Vuolich.*

Next day there follows plentiful conversation. 'Gaily they talked,
as they sat, some late and lazy at breakfast…/Spoke—of noble
ladies and rustic girls their partners.' Philip, the Chartist equali-
tarian, is all for the rustic maiden:

> *Better a cowslip with root than a prize carnation without it.*

The conversation, springy, characterful and high-spirited, pro-
longs itself, and at the end a group of them, Philip among them,
decide to take three weeks off from their books in order to go on a
walking tour, visiting other Highland reading parties as they go.
Airlie and Hobbes and the Tutor remain behind. The holidaying
group returns, somewhat overdue, but Philip is not with them.

73

Where is he? Leaving the others for the moment where they are, Clough addresses his Muse:

> *Thou with thy Poet, to mortals mere post-office second-hand knowledge*
> *Leaving, wilt seek in the moorland of Rannoch the wandering hero.*

Philip, after some tender passages with Katie, a farmer's daughter from the lochside of Rannoch, has left her and is walking the mountains alone. He has seen another girl—'going by in a party with others'—one that he remembers from the clan-gathering at Sir Hector's. The thoughts which come to him are guilt-ridden:

> *Tell me then, why, as I sleep, amid hill-tops high in the moorland,*
> *Still in my dreams I am pacing the streets of the dissolute city,*
> *Where dressy girls slithering by upon pavements give sign for accosting*
> *Paint on their beautiless cheeks, and hunger and shame in their bosoms;*
> *Hunger by drink, and by that which they shudder yet burn for, appeasing,—*
> *Hiding their shame—ah God!—in the glare of the public gas-lights?*

News then reaches the Tutor, busy composing a letter of advice to Philip but not knowing where to send it, that Philip 'was staying at Balloch and was dancing with Lady Maria.' The transition from farmhouse kitchens to silks and salons troubles the Chartist in him. Are perhaps the exploited poor after all inevitable and even necessary?

> *Dig in thy deep dark prison, O miner! and finding be thankful;*
> *Though unpolished by thee, unto thee unseen in perfection,*
> *While thou art eating bread in the poisonous air of thy cavern,*
> *Far away glitters the gem on the peerless neck of a Princess.*

This is now the problem which is preoccupying him and which he poses in a letter to his tutor, ending modestly:

> *But we must live and learn; we can't know all things at twenty.*

October comes, but Philip makes no return to the reading-party and the grave man nicknamed Adam. He has reached the Bothie

74

of Tober-na-Vuolich, found there Elspie, the daughter of the 'thin man clad as a Saxon'. She, he is sure now, is the woman for him if she will have him.

Pretty is all very pretty, it's prettier far to be useful.
No, fair Lady Maria, I say not that; but I will say,
Stately is service accepted, but lovelier service rendered,
Interchange of service the law and condition of beauty.

So the wooing of Elspie goes on. She is doubtful. Would not marriage with Philip be too strenuous a steeplechase, with high class barriers having constantly to be jumped? He overpersuades her and David, her father, agrees to the marriage provided Philip returns first to Oxford and his books for a year, thus allowing the pair of them time to think matters over. In Oxford Philip, 'reading like fury', debates the social question once again with Adam. Adam puts the point of view of age and experience:

When the armies are set in array, and the battle beginning,
Is it well that the soldier whose post is far to the leftward
Say, I will go to the right, it is there I shall do best service?
There is a great Field-Marshal, my friend, who arrays our
    battalions;
Let us to Providence trust, and abide and work in our stations.

But Philip has no patience with this:

I am sorry to say your Providence puzzles me sadly...
Though I mistrust the Field Marshal, I bow to the duty of order.
Yet is my feeling rather to ask, where is the battle?
Yes, I could find in my heart to cry, notwithstanding my Elspie,
O that the armies indeed were arrayed! O joy of the onset!
Sound, thou trumpet of God, come forth, Great Cause, to array
    us,
King and leader appear, thy soldiers sorrowing seek thee.
Would that the armies indeed were arrayed, O where is the
    battle!
Neither battle I see, nor arraying, now King in Israel,
Only infinite jumble and mess and dislocation,
Backed by solemn appeal, 'For God's sake, do not stir, there!'

It is a splendid answer, the answer of youth at all times and in all places to the rueful admonishments of experience; it is Clough's own answer, delivered most belatedly but at last in a strong voice and with head well back, to the black-and-white certainties of Dr Arnold.

> *Philip returned to his books, but returned to his Highlands after;*
> *Got a first, 'tis said; a winsome bride, 'tis certain.*

That is the story. It is a realistic one, and shows that Clough had most of the gifts of the novelist, if lacking that crucial one, the ability to build up tension. His characters are closely observed and well differentiated. Although the background against which they act and react is remote, the early-Victorian reader was made immediately aware that here were contemporary people beset by contemporary problems. True, the word 'pastoral' formed part of the sub-title of the poem, but this was another example of the banter which the so-serious Clough had suddenly discovered in himself a talent for. Here were no stylised shepherds and shepherdesses treading antique measures against a backcloth decorated with urns, colonnades, and tamed natural beauties. Here were lusty, lustful young men who had all read *Past and Present* and who were living in the year of revolutions. Here were young women at last dawningly conscious that ignorance and coy subservience were not going to be considered by them a sufficient stock-in-trade for very much longer: 'But I will read your books, though,/Said she: you'll leave me some, Philip?'

Clough's attitude to women is, indeed, developed at length in the poem. It is a forward-looking attitude, much in advance of his time. There is no parallel in *The Bothie* to the patronising, 'there-there-little-woman' tone of Thackeray or to the maundering protectiveness—not really very different from contempt—which David Copperfield is made to show for Dora. Clough had talked long and seriously with Anne, his gifted, slow-developing sister. The status of women, like the status of the miner, 'eating black bread in the poisonous air of his cavern', needed thinking about. True to his innermost nature, Clough is not prepared to go very far in a hurry. There must always, he thinks, be man's work and woman's work, but the relationship between the sexes must be a partnership, less falsified by coyness on the one hand and condescension on the other. He frowns on 'the fuss about girls, the giggling and toying and coying.' And

>   *...balls, dances and evening parties,*
> *Shooting with bows, going shopping together, and hearing them*
>   *singing,*
> *Dangling beside them, and turning the leaves on the dreary piano,*
> *Offering unneeded arms, performing dull farces of escort,*
> *Seemed like a sort of unnatural up-in-the-air balloon-work...*
> *Utter removal from work, mother-earth, and the objects of living.*

'Eve from his own flesh taken' must become, he thinks, 'a spirit restored to his spirit...Unto the mystery's end sole helpmate meet to be with him,'

> *So feel women, not dolls; so feel the sap of existence*
> *Circulate up through their roots from the far-away centre of all*
>   *things.*

The Bothie is a rough, young, helter-skelter poem. It is an astonishing production to come from a man of twenty-nine, after nine years of overwork coupled with hectic, unhealthy hero-worship, and ten years of brooding, introspective aftermath and spiritual let-down. It is a poem of the morning of life, when the heyday is dancing in the blood, when the mystical union between the self and all the glories of the physical world is not an abstraction to be theorised about but a naked reality. 'Your description of the sky and the landscape,' Thackeray wrote to him, 'and that figure of the young fellow bathing shapely with shining limbs and the blue blue sky for a background—are delightful to me. I can imagine to myself the Goddess of bathing in a sort of shimmer under the water...I have only last night finished my work [the current number of *Pendennis*] and lazing in bed this morning your poem arrived in which I read as far as the Goddess of Bathing, and thought I would write off at once at a heat.'

Many heads have been shaken over the hexameters. If he had had the temerity to anglicise the grave perfection of the Virgilian metre then the least he could have done, it was felt, was take a bit of trouble over it. Who did he think he was, dashing off upwards of two thousand hexameter lines in a month and expecting to get away with it? Anyone who tries to make out that English is a language which takes kindly to hexameters is without question undertaking a very difficult brief, but there is an element of

77

pastiche in *The Bothie* which the hexameters help to bring out, and Clough accommodates his measure marvellously well to the academic, bantering chit-chat and to the porpoise-leapings of his undergraduates in their bathing-pool:

> *Airlie remains, I presume, was the answer, and Hobbes, per-*
> *adventure;*
> *Tarry let Airlie May-fairly, and Hobbes, brief-kilted hero,*
> *Tarry let Hobbes in kilt, and Airlie 'abide in breeches';*
> *Tarry let these and read, four Pindars apiece an it like them!*
> *Weary of reading am I, and weary of walks prescribed us;*
> *Weary of Ethic and Logic, of Rhetoric yet more weary,*
> *Eager to range over heather unfettered of gillie and marquis...*
>
> *There they bathed of course, and Arthur, the Glory of Headers,*
> *Leapt from the ledges with Hope, he twenty feet, he thirty;*
> *There, overbold, great Hobbes from a ten-foot height descended,*
> *Prone, as a quadruped, prone with hands and feet protending;*
> *There in the sparkling champagne, ecstatic, they shrieked and*
> *shouted.*

And there are times when he can make his hexameters sing and paint unforgettable pictures for us:

> *It was on Saturday eve, in the gorgeous bright October,*
> *Then when brackens are changed, and heather blooms are faded,*
> *And amid russet of heather and fern green trees are bonnie;*
> *Alders are green, and oaks; the rowan scarlet and yellow;*
> *One great glory of broad gold pieces appears the aspen,*
> *And the jewels of gold that were hung in the hair of the birch-tree,*
> *Pendulous, here and there, her coronet, necklace, and earrings,*
> *Cover her now o'er and o'er; she is weary and scatters them from*
> *her.*

It was Homer, of course, and not Virgil, that Clough had in mind, and though he would have been the first to brush aside any attempt to compare him with Homer as pompous and over-reaching, yet the verve which drives the poem along is genuinely Homer's. Matthew Arnold, no back-scratcher where poetic values were concerned, thought highly of it. It is in his mind at the end of his lecture on translating Homer, given while he was Professor of Poetry at Oxford. He pays *The Bothie* this tribute: 'His poem, of which I before spoke, has some admirable Homeric qualities; out-of-door freshness, life, naturalness, buoyant rapidity. Some of the expressions in that poem,—*Dangerous Corrievechran. Where roads are unknown to Loch Nevish,*—come back now to my ear with the true Homeric ring.'

There has been a certain amount of speculation about where Clough looked for the human material out of which he shaped the lively young people that play their part in *The Bothie.* But it is not the sort of speculation which is very rewarding if it is entered upon too solemnly or drawn out to too great a length. Any writer who undertakes to put human beings on the page—of a novel, or a play, or a narrative poem like Clough's *Bothie*—must look round at the people he knows or has known to see how far they can help him in his purposes. This is not to say that the familiar prefatory statement, 'All characters fictitious', is a lie put prominently forward in the vain hope of helping the writer wriggle through the close mesh of the law of libel, or that every *roman* is a *roman à clef.* Micawber certainly owes a lot to John Dickens, but John Dickens was infinitely more complicated than Micawber or, come to that, than any character in fiction could ever possibly be. All that can usefully be said on this score is that Clough's imagination played round the personalities of his Oxford friends and of those who joined his Scottish reading-parties, that he took a wry look at himself in the person of Hobbes—Hobbes who was physically big and awkward, as is noted in the diving scene just quoted—and that, almost certainly, Philip Hewson, impulsive, egalitarian, amorous, is an affectionate portrait of Tom Arnold.

Hawkins, the Provost of Oriel, returned to Oxford on October 11, 1848, to find a formal little note awaiting his arrival. '*Ego A.B. A.M. Collegii Socius, resigno omne jus meum quod habeo in Collegio praedicto in manus Praeposito et Sociorum ejusdam. Dat Arthur Hugh Clough.*' 'It rather grieves than surprises me', Hawkins wrote in reply. And certainly it had been clear for several months that Clough was determined to be finished with Oxford. He stayed on in his rooms at 99 Holywell until mid-November wondering what to do with himself. Pupils? A private tutorship? 'Doing the literary' as he called it? Emigrating? He couldn't make up his mind. As for emigrating, Tom Arnold wrote to him from New Zealand to tell him that he looked like being elected Principal of a college in Nelson, and was there any chance of his accepting a

Professorship? 'Do I know anything that will do for the Antipodes?' he wrote in reply. 'I know very little of anything but Latin and Greek. What sort of place is Nelson? I forget where it is...I am ready to look at every new place and likely enough to go to none...Finally, my dear Tom, one lives in the daily possibility of falling in love.' The Holywell lodgings were poky, and he did without a fire. The character-forming morning dips at Parsons Pleasure went on. Perhaps they made living in the daily possibility of falling in love easier to bear.

In January he was in London, where Anne arrived about the 17th ready to embark on a few months' pupil-teacher-training at Borough Road School ('The unruliness of the children at the Boro' Road was very painful', she wrote later). He was negotiating with the Committee about the Headship of University Hall. This was a hall of residence for students of University College, London. The plan was that twenty-five students should live there 'under a degree of discipline' and that it should open in October 1849. The Unitarians had contributed largely to the cost of the building. The institution was not to have any sectarian character, and the committee was anxious to find for the office of principal a man who was *not* a Unitarian. On January 21 Clough was able to write to the Provost of Oriel with the news that he had been offered, and had accepted, the headship of this 'new, quasi-collegiate institution'.

From the time of his appointment—which was not to take effect until October—until early in April he was at home in Vine Street, though he abandoned his filial duties for a few days in February in order to visit Manchester where he met Geraldine Jewsbury—whom the Carlyles always referred to as 'Miss Gooseberry'—and Mrs Gaskell ('neither young nor beautiful; very retiring, but quite capable of talking when she likes'). Comments, both public and private, admiring and not-so-admiring, were coming in on *The Bothie* and on his share of the volume called *Ambarvalia*. Kingsley liked *The Bothie*, and said so in *Fraser's*. J. A. Froude 'found it far more perfect read aloud than read silently'—and this is a good point to be remembered still by anyone who finds the going rough throughout a Scotland hexametrically laid out. The Provost of Oriel told him bluntly that 'there are parts of it rather indelicate; and I very much regretted to find also that there were frequent allusions to Scripture, or rather parodies of Scripture, which you should not have put forth'.

He was back in London early in April, making preparations for a journey to Rome. Anne was still in London, her tough assignment at the Borough Road recently over. 'Arthur does not seem to mind much about people here,' she wrote. 'They don't seem to suit him exactly, and he gets wearied and worn out with the continual talking about religious matters; and I think, too, the pomp and grandeur trouble him. He does not appear at all to fancy coming to live in London.' And there was discussion of much else too, beside religion, while they were both together in London that month. *The Bothie* was a talking point, and the question of the status of women, which bulks so largely in it, was eagerly debated. "I wondered,' Anne wrote, 'to hear Mr Palgrave talk about women as if only those like Lady Maria in Arthur's story were to be admired. I don't much fancy men often understand women; they don't know how restless and weary they get. Arthur was out nearly all of Monday and Tuesday. On the latter day I went to Chelsea to fetch the cigar-case he was to take for Mazzini.'

The cigar-case for Mazzini: Clough was still Citizen Clough, and, even if Lamartine had handed over the republic he spoke so mellifluously about to the opportunist Louis Napoleon, there were other revolutionary spirits abroad and other revolutions brewing. The liberalism with which Pio Nono had begun his long reign in 1846 had been strangled by the assassination of his minister Rossi on November 15, 1848. Abandoning attempts at compromise, Pio escaped from Rome on November 24 and took refuge in the territories of the die-hard King Bomba. Garibaldi, prowling about hungrily in the Apennines with his Legion, awaited a call to Rome from the provisional government. On February 8, 1849, a republic was proclaimed, and in March Mazzini arrived in Rome to form a government. But Pio had other, and stronger, friends than Bomba, and Mazzini was under no delusions about the precariousness of his hold on power.

By the time Clough arrived in Rome on April 16 Mazzini, that morally elevated, deistical, Arnoldian figure, had the fullest need of what soothing comfort he could inhale from the contents of Clough's cigar-case. The Austrians, having defeated the neurotic, liberal Charles Albert of Piedmont at Novara, were pressing southwards in strength. Louis Napoleon, pushed into the Presidency by the French bourgeoisie still terrified by the extremism of Louis Blanc and his followers, had dispatched troops by sea to give support to the exiled Pio Nono. These troops, ten thousand of them under General Oudinot, were within a week of disembarking at Civitavecchia when Clough, shaky after a rough crossing from Marseilles, arrived at the Hotel d'Angleterre. This *putsch*, one of the least creditable episodes in French nineteenth-century history, was justified by the government in Paris on the grounds that French catholic opinion needed to be wooed and that, if, as seemed likely, there was any liberating of Rome to be done in the near future, it was essential that Austria should not be given the chance to do it.

The Hotel d'Angleterre was almost empty. The English tourists, experts now after a year and a half of revolutions at the early diagnosis of a sticky situation, had left the week before. Rome disappointed him. A rubbishy place he called it in a letter to his mother—an epithet that was to remain in his memory. But if it was rubbishy at any rate very soon it was going to be exciting. 'I went up to the Pincian Hill,' he wrote Anne on the 30th, 'and saw the smoke and heard the occasional big cannon and the sharp succession of skirmishers' volleys bang, bang, bang—away beyond St Peter's.' The Romans, with Garibaldi on hand to inject spirit into them, defended themselves valorously on that day. The French had to abandon the idea of settling the matter with a swagger and a brisk single engagement. They withdrew after a mauling; and settled down to a sedate and, by twentieth-century standards most courteous, siege. Clough was there through it all. He was there for the hard fighting of June 3 when Garibaldi, never at his best when his battleground was hemmed in and denied him room to manoeuvre, suffered a check. He was there for the misfortune of the night of June 21—'a very fatal go' as he called it—when the French made a breach in the Roman line, and for the entry of the French troops on the 30th, the resignation of Mazzini and the withdrawal of Garibaldi with his troops to begin the most stirring of all his great marches. 'There is a Mrs Garibaldi,' Clough told Palgrave. 'She went out with him for the Abruzzi. I hope the French won't cut them to pieces, but vice-versa...Last night [he is writing on July 7] I had the pleasure of abandoning a cafe on the entrance of the French.' Although most of the English had left before he arrived, a few, all staunch in their support of the Roman republic, stayed like Clough and saw it through. George Thomas, the artist, was there, making sympathetic drawings of the Garibaldini and sending them home for publication; so was the American Margaret Fuller, comforting the wounded and devoting herself, then as always, to the cause of Mazzini. 'Dear Mr Clough,' she wrote to him at the height of the siege, 'It was very kind of you to give the cologne; there will fall from these bottles many drops of comfort for these hot, tired, but most patient patients...' Clough treasured the note and in 1852 enclosed it in a letter to his future wife: 'Take care of the enclosed, my dearest; and be tender to the memory of the good Margaret.'

In his letters he made light of his own situation, insisting always that he was in no danger. 'We've been bombarded, my dear, think of that', he told Tom Arnold on June 18. 'But it is funny to see how much like any other city a besieged city looks.' He was able to fulfil his duties as a tourist. 'I get on fairly enough—St Peter's and the Sistine Chapel are always available...At last I have got my permit for the Vatican. Once having seen a couple of lines from Mazzini—my goodness how the officials skipped about me.' He also found time to write *Amours de Voyage*, but this activity he kept very much to himself. There is no word about it to anyone in his letters written during the siege. The first mention of it comes in a letter written on October 31 from University Hall.

He began his work there at the beginning of October. He had eleven undergraduates—fewer than had been expected—and one pupil. The buoyancy which had sustained him through the eighteen months which had gone by since his leaving Oriel and which had enabled him to complete two long poems seemed to drop away from him the moment he began tackling his duties as a don in Stinkomalee. 'I shall be kicked out for mine heresies' sake,' he was telling Tom Arnold before he had been there a month. 'I have no confidence in my own tenure. For intolerance, O Tom, is not confined to the cloisters of Oxford or the pews of the establishment, but comes up like the tender herb—partout.' It was a few days after this dispirited outburst that he sent the manuscript of *Amours de Voyage* to Shairp. 'You and Walrond may read this, but don't show it to others, nor therefore name it, as if you do they'll importune.' Shairp, when he replied, could find little in the piece to admire and candidly said so. 'The state of soul of which it is a

83

projection I do not like…everything crumbles to dust beneath a ceaseless self-introspection and criticism…gaiety of manner where no gaiety is, becomes flippancy…This is Beppoish or Don Juanish …On the whole I regard *Les Amours* as your nature ridding itself of long-gathered bile…Don't publish it.' Clough reacted spiritedly to this. 'You're a funny creature, my dear old fellow—if one don't sing you a ballant or read you a philosophic sermonette, if one don't talk about the gowans or faith—you're not pleased.' But perhaps he allowed the criticisms to weigh with him more than he admitted. At all events, if he did not follow Shairp's advice he at any rate followed Pope's in the 'Epistle to Dr Arbuthnot' and kept his piece nine years. It did not appear until 1858, when James Russell Lowell bought it for publication in the *Atlantic Monthly*.

Shairp's sharp shout of disapproval on reading *Amours de Voyage* is not perhaps surprising. Readers, even when they are close friends, always expect a writer to go on doing the same thing, and the *Amours*, except for the hexameters, is very far from being a companion-piece to the *Bothie*. Clough seems to have passed, in order to write these two, from the glad, confident morning of youth to the cynical late afternoon of middle-age all in the space of nine months. In fact, the deflatedness so noticeable in his letters once he was back at University Hall, must have begun to creep over him during those weeks of siege. The spectacle of liberalism taking yet another knock—at the hands of a people who as recently as February 1848 had been so valiant for what he felt to be righteousness; the disappointment at discovering that even the fabled leader, Mazzini, was no more than a poor, forked, fallible human creature (Clough had an interview with him and noted that 'he is a less fanatical fixed-idea sort of man than I had expected; he appeared shifty, and practical enough')—these experiences must have served to remind him that disillusion, listlessness and self-contempt are not banished for ever by the devil-may-care resignation of an Oxford Fellowship.

Clough's novelistic talents, easily discernible in the *Bothie*, are exercised more tellingly in the *Amours*. For action he looks no further than his own situation at the moment of writing. Claude, the English tourist, is besieged in Rome, and writes letters home to Eustace describing the sights, and the ebb and flow of the battles. He also describes the progress of his untempestuous love-affair with Mary Trevellyn who is in Rome with her family—'Middle-class people these,' Claude thinks, 'bankers very likely, not wholly/Pure of the taint of the shop.' He likes Mary but is astonishingly reluctant to let himself go. Falling in love is a serious business and must be thought about. He asks himself endless questions. Are his feelings illusory? Is his emotional state blinding him to the reality that is Mary? Is it worth going ahead with this since after all isn't it extremely likely that Mary has taken a dislike to him? In the middle of his communings the Trevellyns leave Rome, and this decisiveness stirs him at last to decision. Yes, he wants Mary and he must go after her. But these are not normal times. Civil tumult is everywhere and communications are very chancy. He follows up each clue to their whereabouts—Florence, Milan, Bellagio, Como—only to find the Trevellyns gone by the time he gets there. And so, disheartened, Claude gives up his pursuit—'After all, do I know that I really cared so much about her?'

Claude is certainly a change after the headlong, impulsive Philip. Equally certainly he is not a portrait of Clough himself, but rather a projection of part of him just as Philip is a projection of another part—the impetuous part which caused him to go down in William Arnold's *Rules of Football* as 'the best goalkeeper on record', and compounded with much that he saw in Tom Arnold. 'I can be nothing at all if it is not critical wholly'—that is Claude's watchword. He is, of all heroes, the most determinedly unheroic, the most wary-eyed dodger of all forms of enthusiasm. He taps the walls of all the gorgeous palaces man has built for himself—there are plenty awaiting his inspection in Rome—and everywhere the sound he hears is hollow. Man has gone wrong over religion: 'Luther was foolish—but O great God! what call you Ignatius?' The statues of Ceres and Juno and all the ancient gods he sees about him remind him that B.C., as well as A.D., has to have a place in any synthesis

> *Are ye also baptised? Are ye of the kingdom of heaven?*
> *Utter, O someone, the word that shall reconcile Ancient and Modern!*

Aren't all the class-hesitations that he (Claude) is displaying about Mary's tradesman-father contemptible?

Is it contemptible, Eustace—I'm perfectly ready to think so—
Is it—the horrible pleasure of pleasing inferior people?

Isn't this feeling he has for her due to nothing more grandiose or more uplifting than 'Juxtaposition, in short; and what is juxtaposition?' Is there anything, beyond a certain measure of pathos, in the struggles of the 'poor little Roman Republic'? Is there any sense, among so much cynical betrayal on every side, in an individual's sacrificing himself to a cause—any cause?—

> Dulce *it is, and* decorum, *no doubt, for the country to fall,—to*
> *Offer one's blood an oblation to freedom, and die for the Cause;*
> *yet*
> *Still, individual culture is also something, and no man*
> *Finds quite distinct the assurance that he of all others is called on,*
> *Or would be justified even, in taking away from the world that*
> *Precious creature, himself.*

Even though the Garibaldini gain a victory,

> *...smoke of sacrifice rises to heaven,*
> *Of a sweet savour, no doubt, to Somebody; but on the altar,*
> *Lo, there is nothing remaining but ashes and dirt and ill-odour.*

And isn't he right, after all, in his haverings and hesitations about Mary, because may not this attraction which he feels be the wrong kind, the kind that 'simply disturbs, unsettles, and makes you uneasy' as against the other, true sort which 'poises, retains, and fixes and holds you'?

> *I do not like being moved: for the will is excited; and action*
> *Is a most dangerous thing; I tremble for something factitious,*
> *Some malpractice of heart and illegitimate process;*
> *We are so prone to these things, with our terrible notions of duty.*

Here is the Rugby-praepostor-on-the-rebound administering the lie direct to Dr Arnold. Obligation, the spectre that takes shape immediately once a decision has been taken—the decision to commit oneself wholly and avowedly to one woman, for example— is it not wisest to dodge it? Is not evasive action always the safest course when decision-taking and obligation confront one? 'Terrible word, Obligation!' says Claude. '...I will be free in this; you shall not, none shall, bind me.'

86

Clough would never allow himself to become as cynical and as nihilistic as Claude. There was in him a fundamental docility, a fundamental stoicism too, which kept him most of the time busily going through the motions. But what an unforgettably brilliant portrait is his portrait of Claude in *Amours de Voyage*! Here is the man he sometimes—not always—felt himself to be: a crippled, paralysed person, someone who had had the natural, instinctive man in him throttled into lifelessness by too much indoctrination, too much moralising, too much deliberate cultivation and forcing of guilt-feelings, so that any action—even one taken to satisfy his primary, human, sexual needs—became uncertain, hesitant and half-hearted. '*Action will furnish belief*—but will that belief be the true one?'

The hexameters, dashing and headlong in the *Bothie*, are here more pondered, subtler in their effects.

What I cannot feel now, am I to suppose that I shall feel?

How artfully, in a line such as this, is an outlandish metre used to bring out to the full the rhythms and stresses of natural speech. Rome, being fought over but living through it, is brought most vividly before the reader's eyes. The long gaps when there is nothing to do but wait, the guessing, the apparent pointlessness, the sudden, unrelated eruptions of violence—

Passing away from the place with Murray under my arm, and
Stooping, I saw through the legs of the people the legs of a body

—all the immediate indecisiveness of what later turns out to have been decisive is made clear to the reader. What Stendhal does for Waterloo in *La Chartreuse de Parme*, Clough does for the siege of Rome in *Amours de Voyage*. On the whole, of course, it is Clough's intention to make his hexameters talk rather than sing. And this is entirely appropriate to the dominant mood of his poem, which is wry, defeatist and disillusioned.

Rome disappoints me much; I hardly as yet understand, but
Rubbishy *seems the word that most exactly would suit it.*

But there are moments, brief enough, when this mood is laid aside, and then his lines lift effortlessly in response.

Tibur is beautiful, too, and the orchard slopes, and the Anio
Falling, falling yet, to the ancient lyrical cadence;
Tibur and Anio's tide; and cool from Lucretilis ever,
With the Digentian stream, and with the Bandusian fountain,
Folded in Sabine recesses, the valley and villa of Horace...

Sometimes they are wild and convulsive, like a rock-climber, dangling and momentarily helpless, at the end of his sustaining rope:

Lo, with the rope on my loins I descend through the fissure; I sink,
*   yet*
Inly secure in the strength of invisible arms up above me;
Still, wheresoever I swing, wherever to shore, or to shelf, or
Floor of cavern untrodden, shell-sprinkled, enchanting, I know I
Yet shall one time feel the strong cord tighten about me—
Feel it, relentless, upbear me from spots I would rest in; and
*   though the*
Rope sway wildly, I faint, crags wound me, from crag unto crag re-
Bounding, or, wide in the void, I die ten deaths, ere the end I
Yet shall plant firm foot on the broad lofty spaces I quit, shall
Feel underneath me again the great massy strengths of
*   abstraction...*

There is nothing elegant or neatly tailored here. Miss Woodward finds the lines deplorable, but don't they make us see the little figure kicking out wildly at the end of his rope, and don't the flat, firm spondees of 'Yet shall plant firm foot on the broad lofty spaces' slow us down in exactly the right way as the marionette ceases to jig having at last found a foothold?

Shairp thought that the execution was wanting in dramatic power, scenes and scenery, that the analysis was *too absorbing*. Clough, when he replied to this, was 'not sure that Scenes and Scenery, after which you always go awhoring, would exactly improve the matter'. And surely Clough is right. Claude is not a man for scenes. He is the sort of man to come out of it all, not with a bang, not with a whimper either, but with a barely perceptible shrug.

Shall we come out of it all, some day, as one does from a tunnel?
Will it be all at once, without our doing or asking,
We shall behold clear day, the trees and meadows about us,

88

And the faces of friends, and the eyes we loved looking at us?
Who knows? Who can say? It will not do to suppose it.

Shairp liked the conception no better than the execution. 'There is nothing hearty and heart-whole in it,' he told Clough, 'no strength except in its raillery at all men and things and in its keen, ceaseless self-introspection. I do not like the point of view nor atmosphere from which it looks out on the world.' Clough replied to this too, and the reply was spirited. 'Does the last part seem utterly sceptical to your sweet faithful soul?—Goodbye—Your censure of the conception almost provoked me into publishing—because it showed how washy the world is in its confidences...But I probably shan't publish for fear of a row with my Sadducees [the governing body of University Hall].' 'How washy the world is'—this is true and typical of Clough—of the reborn, reinvigorated Clough who walked out of Oriel and scandalised Hawkins by sending him *The Bothie*. In spite of the unrelieved earnestness of his upbringing, in spite of the mood of hushed solemnity which his contemporaries, almost to a man, brought to the business of living, in spite of the glazed, saintly stare with which Clough himself as a Rugby schoolboy fixes us, in spite of the drooping, lily-like, melancholy figure exquisitely if faintly sketched in for us in Arnold's *Thyrsis*—in spite of all this the astonishing fact is that Clough could be a ribald scoffer. The *Amours de Voyage* is *fun*—acrid, bitter, Swiftean fun, if you like, but none the less fun. No poem, speaking to us out of the middle of the last century, catches the mood and enlists the sympathy of our own time as surely and as completely as Clough's *Amours de Voyage*. It is not difficult to understand the headshaking and the swift indrawings of breath with which his contemporaries received it. Even Emerson, one of his staunchest admirers had his doubts. They had accustomed themselves to the idea of a very different kind of Clough—a reverend, dedicated, occasionally whiffling Doubter—a man formed in an image having the widest possible currency in the 'forties and 'fifties of the last century. (It is how people still think of him, in so far as they think of him at all.) It was how Matthew Arnold, a man plentifully gifted indeed, but none the less totally lacking in a sense of humour, thought of him. They were all of them, to a greater or less degree, disconcerted by the *Amours* side of their friend. They tended to shut their eyes, dismiss it, and pretend it never really existed. But it did. It is the side of him which most readily awakens all that is best in him—and there is so much—as a writer. For long stretches of time this *esprit railleur* element in his complicated nature seemed to dive below the surface and run, if it ran at all, underground. But when it was uppermost in him, as it was in the years between leaving Oriel and going to the United States, a very large proportion of his finest work got itself written.

Writing of *Amours de Voyage*, Mr F. L. Lucas has the remark, 'The idea of a novel in hexameter letters hardly stirs the blood.' He goes on, however, to make very ably the point that in Clough's case the idea turns out very much better in practice than in prospect; but his sentence is quoted here, not because, after a growling start, he shows himself to be pro-Clough, but because of his flat, unqualified use of the word 'novel'.

Was Clough a novelist *manqué*—or perhaps not even so very much *manqué*? Or does his work in the *Amours* fall short somewhere in this respect and should he be thought of rather as a verse portraitist attempting a genre successfully worked by Browning in such pieces as 'Fra Lippo Lippi' or 'Bishop Blougram'? The simple mention of two such poems as these, admirable in their kind, makes it immediately clear that Clough's achievement in the *Amours* is something far different, something more complicated, more highly organised, more novelistic. Bishop Blougram is a static, sedentary person. The people in the *Amours* develop and interact. Their affairs reach a climax, however muted and played down this climax may be. There is a story—a wry, inglorious little trickle to be sure, but quite sufficient for, indeed exactly suited to the sort of psychological explorations which Clough was intent on making. Claude, even if he is the chief, is not by any means the only character to be brought into focus. Mary Trevellyn, the girl he dithers over, and Georgina, her vulgar, domineering sister are both brought perfectly to life in a few small subtle strokes, and George Vernon, the Laertes to Claude's Hamlet, is felt as a person throughout, although he never speaks in his own person. Mary, in particular, the decent, inept, blinkered little bourgeoise is presented with astonishing insight. She is too inexperienced to know how to deal with a man who refuses his fences, too inexperienced even to know with any clearness whether she wants him to take them. Yet she is intuitively aware of much in Claude which that bookish intellectual quite fails to see for himself. Here she is writing self-revealingly to her governess:

> *...he does most truly repel me.*
> *Was it to you I made use of the word? or who was it told you?*
> *Yes, repulsive; observe, it is but when he talks of ideas*
> *That he is quite unaffected, and free, and expansive, and easy;*
> *I could pronounce him simply a cold intellectual being.—*
> *When does he make advances?—He thinks that women should woo him;*
> *Yet if a girl should do so, would be but alarmed and disgusted.*
> *She that should love him must look for small love in return; like the ivy,*
> *On the stone wall, must expect but a rigid and niggard support, and*
> *E'en to get that must go searching all round with her humble embraces.*

This is not at all the way in which English novels were being written in 1849. It was a time of broad strokes, simple contrasts and stereotyped formulas. Clough's preoccupation with nuances, his relegation of plain narrative to a subordinate role, and above all the swiftness and economy of the means he employed—the three-decker is cut down to the size of a racing yacht and loses nothing by the change—all these are the characteristics of a very forward-looking novelist indeed. Claude, Murray in hand, dutifully doing his Roman sights in defiance of all alarms and emergencies, is a character Henry James would have warmed to— only James, of course, would have hummed and hawed a lot more over him and blunted by so doing the sharpness of the outline. Clough, in a very few eventful weeks, wrote a small masterpiece. It was unregarded in his own time and it has been undervalued ever since. But for all his susceptibility to the views of others he must have known that he had achieved something good. There is a quiet confidence in the little envoi he wrote for it:

> *So go forth to the world, to the good report and the evil!*
> *Go, little book! thy tale, is it not evil and good?*

Go, and if strangers revile, pass quietly by without answer.
  Go, and if curious friends ask of thy rearing and age,
Say, 'I am flitting about many years from brain unto brain of
  Feeble and restless youths born to inglorious days:
But' so finish the word, 'I was writ in a Roman chamber
  When from Janiculum heights thundered the cannon of France.'

Six

CLOUGH's lack of confidence in his own tenure at University Hall went on growing. After seven months of it he was writing to his mother, who had been wondering about coming to London to join him, in the following hesitant terms: he doubted if she would find it agreeable. 'Dull and dismal as Liverpool is, and little as you may care about people whom you know there, still London is drearier to those who have no old acquaintance in it.' And he doubted the wisdom of moving also because of the uncertainty of his own position. 'I don't *very* much like the situation, to tell you the truth—that is I don't much fancy the *people*.' He learnt, he thought, a lot about life there, and came to realise more and more strongly how unreal and how insulated his Oxford life had been. 'How ignorant,' he told Shairp in June 1850, 'you and I and other young men of our set are. Actual life is unknown to an Oxford student, even though he is not a mere Puseyite and goes on jolly reading parties.' Marriage began to claim his friends. J. A. Froude had been married on October 3, 1849. News came in July 1850 of the engagement of Tom Arnold. 'Matt,' Clough told him in a letter of congratulation, 'is himself deep in a flirtation with Miss Wightman, daughter of a judge.' And Shairp, away in his Highlands, was thinking about it too—perhaps, like Claude, a little too precisely: 'That foolish Shairp will hang on till he is quite bald...putting the pros and cons, and philosophizing about sentiment, till he becomes loathsome to womankind and a burden to himself.' These events and portents increased his sense of loneliness. 'I myself begin to think I shall be a last rose of summer, werry faded.' His friendship with Carlyle—'the cigar-case for

Mazzini' which Anne had gone to Chelsea for before her brother's setting-out for Rome had been, of course, from Carlyle—did something to alleviate his sense of having reached only a temporary halting-place in hostile territory. Carlyle thought highly of him. 'Of Clough,' Froude writes, 'Carlyle had formed the highest opinion, as no one who knew him could fail to do. His pure beautiful character, his genial humour, his perfect truthfulness, alike of heart and intellect—an integrity which had led him to sacrifice a distinguished position and brilliant prospects, and had brought him to London to gather a living as he could from under the hoofs of the horses in the streets—these together had recommended Clough to Carlyle as a diamond sifted out of the general rubbish-heap. But as we have seen, for Clough friendship with Carlyle was not the honour and privilege it might once have been, and the admiration of Carlyle, who had found so much to disapprove of in the events of 1848, not really very precious any more.

The Unitarians at any rate were beginning not to share Carlyle's approval of him. By February 1851, halfway through his second year, stiffish letters were shuttling to and fro between him and his governors. 'I must be pardoned,' he told Martineau, 'if I do not attach the full value of evidence to unauthenticated reports touching either the conduct of any of my pupils or of myself...I was not prepared to recommend to the Council the immediate removal of a Student, because his bill for malt-liquor is large, and because he occasionally plays at cards...Of the steps which I have taken or shall take in this affair I shall of course be ready to give an account to the next Council. May I only once again beg that evidence in the hands of individual members may not then be heard by me for the first time, and I blamed for not having acted on it?' Clough, it is clear from this, had not yet learnt how to handle Councils and Committees. He was young, after all. Their little idiocies and their blustery trump-cards—the same then as now—confused and distressed him. He was not at any time a man with much skill at riding punches. '*I* could have gone cracked at times last year,' he wrote to Tom Arnold on May 16, 1851, 'with one thing and another, I think—but the wheel comes round.'

But in the middle of it, between the end of July and the beginning of October 1850, he went abroad again, crossing first to Antwerp and spending the greater part of his holiday in Venice. He found that the creative spring-tide which had borne him up ever

94

since his break with Oriel had still not begun to ebb. He wrote *Dipsychus*—the double-minded one. As with *The Bothie* and the *Amours* he kept very quiet about it. There is no word from him to anybody of what he is busy with, and indeed few letters of any kind have survived to chronicle this second Italian visit.

Dipsychus has been called his masterpiece because it contains more of himself than any other poem. If one decides—it is a very hard decision—not to attach first importance to his ability to create a world outside himself, to his novelistic ability, then *Dipsychus* might well be allowed to take first place among his works. His gifts for vehement flippancy and mordant satire are never better displayed than here, and the central question of his life—must the inability to believe, or, better, the refusal to force oneself to believe, inevitably result in the total handing over of oneself to the world, the flesh and the devil—receives a characteristically qualified answer—a double-thinking, Cloughian answer:

> *Be it then thus—since that it must, it seems.*
> *Welcome, O world, henceforth; and farewell dreams!*
> *Yet know, Mephisto, know, nor you nor I*
> *Can in this matter either sell or buy;*
> *For the fee simple of this trifling lot*
> *To you or me, trust me, pertaineth not.*
> *I can but render what is of my will,*
> *And behind it somewhat remaineth still...*

Dipsychus was not published in Clough's lifetime. It w printed from manuscript drafts. It is a rough, bitter, tormented, naïve poem, the work of someone becoming aware of himself as a stunted tree in danger of withering, of someone who realises that the instinctive, natural man in him has been planed away to nothingness by the forces of education and upbringing. It is cast in the form of a series of conversations between Dipsychus and the 'Spirit'. This Spirit is reluctant to fix his identity within the bounds of a single name. Mephistophilis? Belial?—

> *But take your pick; I've got a score—*
> *Never a royal baby more.*
> *For a brass plate upon the door*
> *What think you of* Cosmocrator?

Cosmocrator—the Power of this World—will have to do for him.

He is gay and beautifully articulate. At least one of the many Cloughs must have loved writing his part for him:

> This world is very odd we see,
>   We do not comprehend it;
> But in one fact we all agree,
>   God won't, and we can't mend it.
> Being common sense, it can't be sin
>   To take it as I find it;
> The pleasure to take pleasure in;
> The pain, try not to mind it.

The dramatic form which Clough adopts proves at least one point conclusively, however much it may wriggle and hedge over all others, that Clough, however golden his future as a novelist might have been, would never have made a playwright. The first scene takes place in the piazza at Venice at 9 p.m. Dipsychus is brooding over a poem written a year earlier—Easter Day, Naples 1849. He quotes it—it is, of course, an actual poem of Clough's and one well worth quoting.

> Through the great sinful streets of Naples as I passed,
>   With fiercer heat than flamed above my head
> My heart was hot within me; till at last
>   My brain was lightened when my tongue had said—
>   Christ is not risen!

The Spirit mocks him for his worries over what he has said, for his 'thing ill-worked—A moment's thought committed on the moment', and tells him to 'enjoy the minute'. The Spirit then tries to make a social man out of him. Dipsychus, with his 'o'er-discernment', finds it difficult 'to herd with people that one owns no care for/To drain the heart with endless complaisance'. The Spirit tells him not to fuss. He

> ...quite can think our modern parties pleasant.
> One shouldn't analyse the thing too nearly:
> The main effect is admirable clearly.

Then Dipsychus is on the piazza again. He has been insulted by a German officer—or perhaps he was a Croat. 'Go up to him!' urges the Spirit, '—you must, that's flat./Be threatened by a beast like that!' But there are no simple issues for Dipsychus.

> *Instinct turns instinct out, and thought*
> *Wheels round on thought.*

He has plentiful reasons for doing nothing, sufficient delaying arguments to blunt the Spirit's natural-man reactions. They make an excursion to the Lido where Dipsychus indulges in Timon-like railings and the Spirit sings a disillusioned little ditty by way of coda.

> *'There is no God,' the wicked saith,*
> *'And truly it's a blessing,*
> *For what He might have done with us*
> *It's better only guessing'...*
> *But country folks who live beneath*
> *The shadow of the steeple;*
> *The parson and the parson's wife,*
> *And mostly married people;*
> *Youths green and happy in first love,*
> *So thankful for illusion;*
> *And men caught out in what the world*
> *Calls guilt, in first confusion;*
> *And almost everyone when age,*
> *Disease or sorrows strike him,*
> *Inclines to think there is a God,*
> *Or something very like Him.*

Then follow two songs, the gondola-song which is as singable a lyric as he ever wrote, and that brisk, satirical gallop round the fleshpots which concludes with the stanza:

> *They may talk as they please about what they call pelf,*
> *And how one ought never to think of oneself,*
> *And how pleasures of thought surpass eating and drinking—*
> *My pleasure of thought is the pleasuring of thinking*
> *How pleasant it is to have money, heigh ho!*
> *How pleasant it is to have money.*

After the singing comes the brooding, the analysis of the warring elements in himself which hinder action, the hesitations at which the Spirit jeers:

> *'...past other men*
> *To cherish natural instincts, yet to fear them*
> *And less than any use them.'*

97

The Spirit calls on him to submit:

> '...*in earth's great laws*
> *Have you found any saving clause,*
> *Exemption special granted you*
> *From doing what the rest must do?'*

But Dipsychus is not yet ready for this. To submit, after all, is to decide, and for him, with his neurotic itch always to remain uncommitted, decisions are the hardest things of all.

> '...*Is it a law for me*
> *That opportunity shall breed distrust,*
> *Not passing until that pass?'*

He falls asleep, exhausted by all the marching and counter-marching he has had to do in order to remain in the same place, and Cosmocrator, or Cosmarchon, or perhaps just plain Belial muses over him contemptuously—

> '...*Methinks I see you*
> *Twirling and twiddling ineffectively*
> *And indeterminatedly swaying for ever.'*

—knowing that submission, even if to the end pathetically quali-fied, will have to come.

There is a prose prologue to *Dipsychus* in which the poet's uncle is represented as composing himself for a hearing of what is to follow, and as urging the young fellow to get started—'while Aristarchus is tolerably wakeful'. Now, the submission made, uncle and poet walk on the stage again in a prose epilogue. What the uncle has been witnessing has been the conflict between a tender conscience and the world—an over-tender one, perhaps, which the devil was quite right to be brusque with? 'Consciences,' the uncle agrees, 'are often much too tender in your generation. It's all Arnold's doing; he spoilt the public schools...How often have I not heard from you, how he used to attack offences, not as offences—the right view—against discipline, but as sins, heinous guilt, I don't know what beside. Why didn't he flog them and hold his tongue? Flog them he did, but why preach?' If there was error in the Arnoldian system, the poet thinks, it should be ascribed to the spirit of the time rather than to Arnold. Here the debate is dropped. As the passage is written, there can be no question that it is the uncle, and not the poet, who has the better of the argument. 'Good night, dear uncle,' the poet concludes. 'Only let me say you six more verses.' These six verses spread into four scenes in which Dipsychus is seen thirty years later talking to a prostitute he consorted with in his youth. He dismisses her on the plea of court business though she is eager to talk to him on matters which remain unspecified. In court Dipsychus has a seizure, and after he has been carried away the barristers talk him over:

> '*My father knew him at college: a reading man,*
> *The quietest of the quiet—shy and timid;*
> *And college honours past,*
> *No one believed he ever would do anything.*'
> '*He was a moral sort of prig, I've heard,*
> *Till he was twenty-five; and even then*
> *He never entered into life as most men.*
> *That is the reason why he fails so soon.*
> *It takes high feeding and a well-taught conscience*
> *To breed your mighty hero of the law.*
> *Indeed,* sine Venere et Libero friget Themis.'

Why did Clough keep so quiet about *Dipsychus*? Perhaps he thought it too incomplete to count. There are four sources for the poem as we have it. The first is a rough draft, almost certainly completed in Venice in 1850. There are many gaps in this, and plentiful variants. The second is a first revision. The opening sections are missing from this, but it contains, and is the only one of the MSS to contain, the epilogue. The third is a second revision which has the prologue (found nowhere else) and a further thousand or so lines which roughly complement the first revision. The fourth is a small book of thirty-six pages which contains a fair copy of much of the first four scenes. The last three of these MSS were worked on either in Venice or immediately on returning home before the beginning of the term at University Hall. They were laid aside then and never returned to. Blanche Smith, his future wife, wrote to him on December 2, 1852: 'Will you please to give me leave to read Dipsychus, for I want to. I have put some of my books in that box and I fetch them out sometimes, and sometimes peep in them and read your Atheistic Song, so please write and tell me to read it all.' He answered: 'Dear Blanche,

please don't read Dipsychus yet—I wish particularly not. You shall
see it sometime—but now, not, please—dear, I beg not, please...'
Blanche, when she was preparing the *Letters and Remains* for the
edition of 1865, had to make of the different bits and pieces as
coherent a whole as she could; she was doubtful, even after that,
whether she ought to publish it, and did in fact suppress a considerable amount of material which is, considering the date at
which it was written, quite remarkably candid about sexual matters.

> *'I know it's mainly your temptation*

says the Spirit

> *'To think the thing a revelation,*
> *A mystic mouthful...*
> *I tell you plainly that it brings*
> *Some ease; but the emptiness of things...*
> *Is the sole lesson you'll learn by it—*
> *Still you undoubtedly should try it...*

'Could I believe' says Dipsychus,

> *'Could I believe that any child of Eve*
> *Were formed and fashioned, raised and reared for nought*
> *But to be swilled with animal delight*
> *And yield five minutes' pleasure to the male—*

And a little further on the Spirit brings in details which come
perhaps more from memory than from imagination:

> *'...if 'twere only just to see*
> *The room of an Italian fille,*
> *'Twere worth the trouble and the money.*
> *You'll like to find—I found it funny—*
> *The chamber où vous faites votre affaire*
> *Stand nicely fitted up for prayer;*
> *While dim you trace along one end*
> *The Sacred Supper's length extend.*
> *The calm Madonna o'er your head*
> *Smiles, con bambino, on the bed...'*

Dipsychus, like the *Amours*, is a poem about human action and
the conditions governing it. Always Clough is conscious of a
tension within himself. The instinctive, natural man pulls one
way: he wants to jump into bed with an Italian fille, he wants to

repay immediately in kind when the brawling foreign soldier lays a hand on him, he doesn't object so much to a flogging but deplores the copious elbow-grease which Dr Arnold expends beforehand in giving a high surface-polish to all guilt-complexes. The conditioned man on the other hand, the successor of the boy who had sat too long and listened too hard in Rugby Chapel, pulls another way: he must be given time to think everything over, time to satisfy himself that each action conforms to pattern, furthers the requirements of a moral order, and satisfies the notions of duty implanted in him—by God? or simply by Dr Arnold?

This tug-of-war leads to deadlock. The only solution must lie in keeping action, outwardness, to a minimum. Carlyle's gospel of work becomes as unacceptable as any other gospel. Carlyle, in fact, was no good any more, and hadn't Emerson consecrated him (Clough) Bishop in his place? In fact no workable course of action is left to the poet, except a gesture of rejection and a turning-in upon the self.

O let me love my love unto myself alone,
And know my knowledge to the world unknown;
No witness to the vision call,
Beholding, unbeheld of all;
And worship thee, with thee withdrawn, apart,
Whoe'er, whate'er thou art,
Within the closest veil of mine own inmost heart.

Better it were, thou sayest, to consent,
Feast while we may, and live ere life be spent;
Close up clear eyes, and call the unstable sure,
The unlovely lovely, and the filthy pure;
In self-belyings, self-deceivings roll,
And lose in Action, Passion, Talk, the soul.

Nay, better far to mark off thus much air
And call it heaven, place bliss and glory there;
Fix perfect homes in the unsubstantial sky,
And say, what is not, will be by-and-by;
What here exists not, must exist elsewhere.
But play no tricks upon thy soul, O man;
Let fact be fact, and life the thing it can.

And all the way through this stoical impasse, this paralysis of his, is mocked by the Spirit, who hammers away at the single point that the world can be all right for the untenderised conscience, so why all the fuss? Why shy away, thinks Dipsychus, from this voice which has all its answers pat? It may well, of course, be the voice of the Devil, if only because it sings all the best tunes (Clough's verve and bite and bitter fun give immense strength and persuasiveness to the part he writes for his Spirit), but God and Devil are both elusive concepts. Perhaps they are not running rival concerns any more but have negotiated a merger?

In the rough draft of the poem and in the first revision the two characters are called respectively Faustulus and Mephisto. Quite clearly when he sat down to write Clough had Goethe in mind, and in his always modest way ('Faustulus' instead of 'Faust') might have thought that by the time he came to the end he might be in a position to invite comparisons with him. Goethe's thought influenced Clough deeply. Goethe's line 'Wen Gott betrügt ist wohl betrogen' haunted him. Goethe's conception of God, as it is expounded for us in *Faust*, is one with which Clough felt close sympathy; Goethe's idea that the Name was nothing, the intimation everything, was one which Clough longed to accept:

> *Aimless and hopeless in my life I seem*
> *To thread the winding byways of the town,*
> *Bewildered, baffled, hurried hence and thence.*
> *All at cross-purpose ever with myself,*
> *Unknowing whence from whither. Then, in a moment,*
> *At a step, I crown the Campanile's top,*
> *And view all mapped below: islands, lagoon,*
> *An hundred steeples and a million roofs,*
> *The fruitful champaign, and the cloud-capt Alps,*
> *And the broad Adriatic...*
> *I am contented, and will not complain.*
> *To the old paths, my soul! Oh, be it so!*
> *I bear the workday burden of dull life*
> *About these footsore flags of a weary world,*
> *Heaven knows how long it has not been; at once,*
> *Lo! I am in the Spirit on the Lord's day*
> *With John on Patmos...*

No one, of course, is going to claim that Clough's *Dipsychus* can stand shoulder to shoulder with Goethe's *Faust*. Clough lacked Goethe's enormous appetite for life. The limitations of his nature are such that he would always have lacked it, however long his life might have been and whatever luck or ill-luck might have had in store for him. He lacked Goethe's breadth and variety of experience which give to *Faust* its stamina and ultimate serenity. He rings down the curtain on a discord and leaves the reader to search for a resolution for himself. Clough's poem is tentative and somehow deflationary compared with Goethe's because Clough cannot bring himself to believe—much as he longed to believe—that divinity inheres not so much in reason as in will. But all this does not make of *Dipsychus* any the less shiningly honest, any the less moving a poem when Faustulus is speaking, or any the less pointed a satire when Mephisto is holding the stage.

The numbers in University Hall stuck obstinately at twelve. The Council of Management made no secret of their opinion that the Principal ought not to turn up his nose at the role of recruiting sergeant. But Clough did not respond. Twelve there were, and twelve, so far as he could see, there would continue to be. Towards the end of 1851 he decided to offer himself as candidate for a classical Professorship at the new university in Sydney. Hawkins wrote coldly from Oriel to say he could not back him. The Thirty-nine Articles still rankled. In spite of this he persisted with his application and so far as backing was concerned made do with what, in the dotty eyes of the world, was very much of a second-best—a testimonial from Matthew Arnold. The University Hall governors got wind of his application, and seem to have decided that this would provide an excuse for getting rid of an unsatis-factory principal. Clough had stated in his application that if appointed he would be willing to leave his post in London in February 1852. At a meeting of the governors on December 11, 1851 it was decided to ask him immediately for an absolute and not a provisional resignation. His rooms at University Hall were put at his disposal till the end of the session, and this guber-natorial grace-and-favour Clough was glad to accept, more especially as the Sydney post failed to come his way.

It was not at all a good moment to lose one job and fail to find another. Earlier in that year, 1851, he had met someone who was as strongminded as Dr Arnold and who was to influence him almost as drastically. He had met Florence Nightingale. Through her he had made the acquaintance of her cousin, Blanche Smith, daughter of Samuel Smith of Tapton and his wife who was Miss Nightingale's famous, too devoted, 'Aunt Mai'. Clough and Blanche Smith became engaged, and they were both eager— Clough was by this time thirty-two—that the engagement should not be a long one. An almost penniless, about-to-be-sacked university teacher was contemplating an alliance with the limitlessly wealthy Nightingale–Smith families. The statistically-minded Miss Nightingale busily worked out minimum budgets for them, but her minima, based on her thirty years' experience of life in the great houses of Victorian England, were well beyond the most optimistic maximum that Clough could stretch to. Conquering his distaste, he devoted himself to lobbying and place-hunting. Lady Ashburton interceded with Lord Lansdowne on his behalf to see if an examinership in the Education Office might not be found for him. He wondered about the chair of Humanity in the University of Aberdeen. But the end of March came, and still there was nothing except for an odd pupil or two from University Hall. Bagehot, through whom it had been chiefly that Clough had been put in the way of the Principalship, showed no pique at the briefness of Clough's tenure. He told R. H. Hutton, his successor at Gordon Square, that Clough had 'never understood a shopkeeper who had been "carefully brought up" ', and thought that Hutton, understanding such governors better, might have more success. Bagehot was also pleased that the Sydney post had fallen through; he did not like the thought of exile for Clough.

But Clough was beginning to think very seriously of exile none the less. May came in and found him still searching, and on the fourteenth he wrote to Blanche: '...We shall be parted, my dear Blanche; it is no use...I see no prospect or hope of anything—and separation, at any rate for sometime, is inevitable in consequence... You see that really with Education for my profession I have so far less chance than others in their professions or in this—because of the stigma of the abjured XXXIX articles...' Clough's thoughts were turning to America, and in particular to Emerson with whom he had kept up the friendship formed first at Oxford and then in Paris in 1848. He wrote to him in June to ask 'Is there any chance, do you think, of earning bread and water, if not bread and flesh, anywhere between the Atlantic and the Mississippi, by teaching Latin, Greek, or English? Emerson was welcoming. 'Do you take the first ship or steamer for Boston,' he replied on July 14, 'come out and spend two or three months here in my house. I will defend you from all outsiders, initiate you step by step into all the atrocities of republicanism.' It seemed best to accept. The examinership in the Education Office which Lady Ashburnham might have worked for him with Lord John Russell in office became very problematic once Derby had formed his first Cabinet in February 1852. A faint hope of a Roman Catholic inspectorship appeared, and he wrote to Ward, now at Old Hill House, Ware, to enlist his support. 'If it would be of any service,' Ward wrote, 'I should be most delighted to bear any amount of testimony on your behalf', but went on to make it clear that no amount of testimony from him could conceivably be of the slightest service. Clough comforted Blanche in her distress at the coming parting. ('Dear child,' he calls her. She was twenty-four.) He arranged about a sailing, made a little pilgrimage to Laleham, 'looked in at the church window' there and 'made out the pulpit where he [Dr Arnold] used to fulminate', and at the beginning of November went aboard the *Canada*, half sailing-ship, half steamer, bound for Cambridge, Massachusetts, and the land of his boyhood.

Seven

WHEN the infrequent fit was on him, Clough wrote fast. In Venice in the summer of 1850 he went at it with the singleminded energy of a dive-bombed soldier pioneering a slit-trench for himself, and wrote what we have of *Dipsychus*, a poem eighty-odd pages long, in a matter of weeks. After the outpouring came the return, not to idleness but to the routine tasks which he always seemed to welcome as offering balm to limbs wearied after a sortie into harsh and hostile territory. Clough's creativeness was the sulky, shy, retiring sort that liked to lock itself away and not reappear unless coaxed out of its *querencia* by some liberating agent. The liberating agent for Clough was always—at any rate during these, the best years of his writing life—a decision. Always, for the first weeks after coming to a conclusion, after going about on a fresh tack, Clough wrote copiously and often well.

Once he was in his 'little coffin of a berth' on the *Canada*, and once he had got over his sea-sickness which lasted four days, the weather being 'horridly awkward', Clough became once again, for a brief spell, a busy writer. He wrote upwards of a dozen lyrics on his way across. For the most part they are love poems addressed to Blanche waiting at home until he could prove himself capable of earning the £500 a year which Samuel Smith not unreasonably fixed as the minimum for the husband of any daughter of his. They are flat and naïve and honest and not very good.

> *Green fields of England! wheresoe'er*
> *Across this watery waste we fare,*
> *Your image at our hearts we bear,*
> *Green fields of England, everywhere.*

Sweet eyes in England, I must flee
Past where the waves' last confines be,
ere your loved smile I cease to see,
Sweet eyes in England, dear to me.

Some are worse than this. Some are very bad indeed, so bad that it is a pity that Blanche, after he was dead, saw fit to publish them. Clough had superb novelistic gifts; the vigour and effectiveness of his mockery and satire were altogether exceptional in that solemn age; he could write a poem like *Easter Day* in which the strength of his intellectual passion asserted itself masterfully; but poetry arising out of a direct relationship, physical as much as spiritual, between himself and another—this he could not manage. To express what was in him in this line the situation had always to be exteriorised: he had to talk through Claude or through Philip. The best thing that can be said for these pieces is that they prove once again that no more unswervingly honest a man than Clough ever put pen to paper.

I knew it when we parted, well,
I knew it, but was loth to tell;
I knew before, what now I find,
That out of sight was out of mind.

That friends, however friends they were,
Still deal with things as things occur,
And that, excepting for the blind,
What's out of sight is out of mind.

But love is, as they tell us, blind;
So out of sight and out of mind
Need not, nor will, I think, be true,
My own and dearest love, of you.

'Need not, nor will, I think, be true'—one must respect him for his inflexible refusal ever to overstate a case. But it is not the way Burns would have talked to a young woman.

Thackeray and Lowell made the crossing to America on the same boat. Lowell in particular was most friendly. *The Bothie* had made a much stronger impression in America than England, and to his surprise Clough found himself being talked about as of someone having a literary stature comparable with Thackeray's. Clough was too much of a puritan, too little a man of the world, to be entirely happy in the company of Thackeray, but it was doubtless agreeable to be associated with him in this way.

When he reached Boston he discovered for himself that Lowell's recognition of him on board had not been by any means a private Lowellian fad. 'In Bosting I am Mr Clow or Clou the *celebrated* author of "the Bothie", a whole edition of which was printed and *sold* (they say) here. Dear me!...' At Cambridge, Massachusetts, he found that 'people here put the poor old Bothie on their drawing-room tables—even at Ticknor's for example, I saw it, last night.'

Clough reached New England at the beginning of a boom decade. The population was to double between 1850–1860. The Year of Revolutions in Europe had produced a problem which was to become more and more familiar in the Old World as the decades rolled by—that of displaced persons. These flooded into the Eastern, especially the North-Eastern states of the Union and—oh sacrilege—into the demure privacies of Massachusetts. They brought a babel of languages with them. Clough tells Carlyle how 'a new language is springing up'. He calls it Anglo-American-Deutsch and notes how an early morning visitor can be asked 'Hast du ge-breakfasted'. They caused serious problems, as immigrants in bulk must inevitably do. The entrenched and exclusive inhabitants of Boston and Cape Cod wrinkled their noses and mostly disapproved.

Their disapproval was natural enough. Boston and Cambridge were in the process of turning themselves into strong and thriving centres of an indigenous American culture, consciously divergent from European modes and traditions. Clough had the entrée into that exclusive intellectual society, probably more unreservedly and for a longer period than any other Englishman of his time.

Slavery was the dominant public issue. Harriet Beecher Stowe's *Uncle Tom's Cabin* came out in 1852. No prim, civilised exclusive New Englander could hold himself aloof from the black man's monstrous wrongs after that. Clough met Mrs Stowe at dinner with the Longfellows. 'I liked her very well,' he told Blanche. 'She has none of the stiffness of the picture I have seen of her...She is small and quite unobtrusive, but quick and ready-witted enough.'

Opinion in Boston wasn't of course unanimous for Abolition. 'The tip-top conservative set,' as Clough calls them—the Ticknors and the Dwights most notably—were 'high Whigs, which means Tories, and quite aristocratic.' They feared for the prosperity of Boston's industrial interests if the cheapness of its basic raw material—cotton—became endangered from want of cheap slave labour. Against the reactionaries were ranged two schools of thought: the out and out Abolitionists, and the Free-Soilers. The gap between these two was not wide. Lowell, Howe and Sumner were Abolitionists: that is to say, they felt that the abolition of slavery should be total, immediate and unconditional. The demands of the moral law could admit of no compromise. The Free-Soilers, while accepting that the case for abolition was un-answerably strong, claimed that questions of timing, of political expediency, could not be left entirely out of account. 'Emerson is a Free-Soiler,' Clough tells Blanche, and Clough himself, noticing that 'there is a great deal of party feeling, malice, envy, hatred, etc. etc.', and having an outsider's ignorance of a long and complicated history of deep antagonisms, seems to have taken the Emerson line. 'If I were to be anything, I should be a Free-Soiler, which only means that you won't have any new Slave States. I wouldn't interfere with existing Slave-States except to intimate that the Central Government is ready to assist in any measure any Slave-State will propose for getting rid of slavery—i.e. to give compensation, etc.'

On the whole Clough did not find the cushioned, luxurious life of the Boston magnates much to his taste. Ticknor, the historian of Spanish literature, and Prescott, the historian of the Conquista-dores, inhabited a golden world of privilege. 'Prescott...has a sickly wife, and lives a good deal in his study. I ought to have taken an introduction to him: for though the Lyells did take me, it didn't seem that he thought it the same thing. People say however that he is a little indolent and self-indulgent in his ways—he's more of a gentleman in his manners than Ticknor but Ticknor is kinder ...There is no *stiffness* here I think; the magnates are a little chilly and constrained at first, perhaps, but that is all fair...' And, in spite of the poor old Bothie's being on display in Ticknor's drawing-room, 'I am not at all a distinguished literary man in the eyes of Ticknor or Prescott, you know.'

He found their womenfolk a bit trying too. He never liked blue-stockings and aspirants to the role of *salonière*. 'For Mrs Ticknor I have no liking...ambitious or pretentious or something or other.'

Or after a little tea-party early in December 1852 he tells Blanche: 'Last night I went to tea at Mrs Ward's. Mrs Ward I like but her friends are offensive to me; they are Margaret Fuller's set I believe, and they do the satirical, and the sarcastic, and the ill-natured, and the fastidious, and the intellectual, and all that—for which one had better go back to London.'

Of the Bostonians Lowell and Longfellow were the ones he found most sympathetic. It was Lowell who saw most clearly Clough's quality as a writer, and Clough was human enough to respond to this. In his first journal-letter to Blanche from Boston he writes: 'Thackeray of course was drunk...Then Mr Degen proposed Lowell, the American poet, and Lowell, in returning thanks, proposed the English poet, me, and all the people stared at this extraordinary piece of information.' Longfellow invited him frequently out to Cambridge. 'I am glad you like Longfellow as a man,' Shairp writes to him, 'though I should have thought from his books he would [not] have suited you! They are too sugarry for me, not to say you, but I'm glad you like the man.' How could he not like him? His warmth and friendliness were a constant comfort. '9 p.m.,' he notes on April 27, 1853, 'I had my class in Ethics and went on with the Article, when Longfellow came in, and asked me to come and dine, which I did, and sat with him afterwards in his balcony, reading English papers.' And many years later Longfellow remembered 'his gentleness and his bewildered look, and his half-closed eyes.' Charles Eliot Norton, active and prosperous in business as well as enthusiastic for learning, was another friend who remained a friend long after the American hegira was over. Norton, eight years younger than Clough, and bringing to their association that touch of discipleship which Clough was often capable of inspiring in his juniors and coevals, invited him frequently to the family estate, Shady Hill in Cambridge, and it was here indeed that Clough spent the last three weeks of his stay in America.

Something under twenty miles from Boston was Concord, where Thoreau brooded and meditated. 'I saw him and the site of his hut by Walden Pool, when I was at Concord. It is not *deep* in the woods, by any manner of means. Were it not real natural forest, known to have supplied the settlers with fuel, and to have been held in wood lots by the colonists (or citizens) of Concord from time immemorial, one could call it a plantation.' Here

Emerson, not really happy on the high social altitudes where the Bostonian Ticknors and Prescotts browsed, dominated all thinking. To Clough he wasn't quite the same Emerson he'd known a few years before in London and Paris. 'With Emerson I spent about four days only,' Clough tells Carlyle in December 1852; 'he is gone away west for the lecture season at Cincinnati and St Louis. Concord is a barish country village—(the houses here have nothing like English gardens)—with three churches, a brick town-meeting house, and lots of white wooden houses, all tidy, all unsubstantial. Emerson lives under a few pines! His mother is a fine old lady—very like him. I find him altered from what he was in England—whether the effect of time or difference of place, I don't know. He seems to have much more of a made-up mind than I thought he had then—with plenty of common-sense for all the ordinary matters of New England life.' Still, altered or not, Clough's high regard for him did not waver. He seems certainly to have found shortcomings in the home life of the Emersons because the sage's second wife was more impractical and out-of-this world than was altogether tolerable: 'a Swedenborgian, I am told. She is not a very good housekeeper, I should say; and I am not sorry to be spared the month's stay there which I had been invited to.' But Emerson himself remained the source of inspiration and spiritual comfort he had always been—'the only profound man in this country.' Concord the place, however—what it stood for, the people who lived there—had its head too much in the clouds for his liking. 'A pokey sort of place,' he told Carlyle, 'and though it has an advantage in being out of the great thoroughfare of trade and dollar-making, it aggravates the tendency to what you call Gymnosophism.'

He found lodgings in Cambridge with Mrs Samuel Howes, 2 Garden Street, at two and a half dollars a week. He was abstemious ('The best drink for this climate is cocoa.'), he watched his money, and touted for pupils. On December 7, at 11.30 in the morning, he sat down with his first pupil, blue-blooded Lindell Winthrop, aged seventeen: 'a long youth, and lazy, but of an easy sort of temper.'

The pupils came and went. It seems to have been a hand-to-mouth business. He thought hard about Lowell's suggestion that he should start a school, but nothing came of it. By March 6, 1853, he had earned the sum of forty-five dollars only. It would be a long time, at this rate, before Samuel Smith gave him the all-clear which would allow him to march ahead into matrimony. He wrote almost daily to Blanche, letters full of financial calculations and unhappiness. 'I fear I am living a very idle useless life here; for my pupil doesn't come at present,' he told her at the turn of the year, 'and I do very little but write to you...Blanche dearest, I hope if you were to live with me and help me, I should get on better, and be better too—I get wrong with people and have nobody to be quite right with—never had so far as I know. I don't know that you would always understand exactly what my little troubles might be, my dear child, but I think I should be right with you; and there is no one else that I can say so of...' He wrote her a revealing one on January 24. 'Why do I write you nice letters (usually) you ask—whereas with you I was uncertain and inexpressive.' It was exactly the sort of question one would have expected a girl to put to him. Early in 1853, perhaps in response to the dejected letter of December 30, quoted above, Blanche must have written offering to come to America. This provoked him to a typical, scrupulous, havering reply. 'One thing that makes me reluctant for you to *come* out, is that I think you ought to have another look at me before you decide to unite your fortunes with my very indifferent fortunes, and give your happiness to my perhaps undesirable keeping.'

Why did he devote himself with such persistence to the un-rewarding trade of tutoring? 'Teaching Greek', he once told Blanche in justification, 'is a very *innocent* trade at any rate—as innocent I should think as most.' But Clough, in America if not in England, was a writer with an established reputation. Wouldn't he have been better employed on another long-vacation pastoral, or another verse-novel shedding light on another emotional no-thoroughfare?—instead of wrestling with a reluctant young Winthrop who had no time for Sophocles but wanted to go filibustering in Cuba. Clough did not forget that it was possible to earn money with a pen as well as with chalk and duster—there was the recent example of Thackeray, waving his princely cheques about on the *Canada* to remind him—but, most mysteriously, all he could do in the literary line was turn himself into a hack. 'My fancy at present,' he told Blanche on January 22, 'is if possible to live here in an humble way, take two or three pupils, and do book-sellers' work, or lecture and so make up an income.' The book-sellers' work was to take the form of helping toward the republishing of Langhorne's Plutarch, and he was to be paid a fee of 350 dollars. It was meagre pay for much hard, humble work. Utterly lacking in ambition though he was, he yet somehow felt that this Grub Street toil needed justifying. 'I am, my dear Blanche, I know and confess, sometimes carried away into a world of abstraction... But surely I am not likely to be *able*, did I wish it, to stay there long...Yet I am always so glad to come away from it. It is odd how much better I like this Plutarch than I do anything which requires distinct statement of opinion or the like.' And again a fortnight later: '...apropos of this Plutarch. It seems to me sometimes as if I must not trifle away time in anything which is not really a work to some purpose.' For Clough the act of creation must have been a greater ordeal than it is for most; he had to screw his courage to the sticking place for a long time before he could bring himself to plunge into those deep and dizzying waters. Indeed it usually needed some force outside himself, some shove from behind, to set him going. Is it fanciful to see here a parallel between Housman and Clough—both classical scholars of the greatest distinction and infrequent, lonely poets—Housman retreating for long years at a time to the safe stronghold of Manilius and Clough cobbling away at Langhorne's Plutarch in his little room in Cambridge, Massachusetts?

Some reviewing for the *North American Review*, in the ample, mid-nineteenth century manner, did come his way, and an original piece, called 'Two Letters of Parepidemus', was published in *Putnam's Monthly* for July and August 1853. These fifty-odd pages of prose were all that Clough the writer had to show for his seven and a half months' stay in America. His longest article was a review of some poems by Alexander Smith and Matthew Arnold, and this has some sentences very characteristic of the author of the *Bothie* and the *Amours*. '...poetry should deal more than at present it usually does, with general wants, ordinary feelings, the obvious rather than the rare facts of human nature.' 'There are moods when one is prone to believe that, in these last days, no longer by "clear spring or shady grove", no more upon any Pindus or Parnassus, or by the side of any Castaly, are the true and lawful haunts of the poetic powers; but, we could believe it, if anywhere, in the blank and desolate streets, and upon the solitary bridges of the midnight city, where Guilt is, and wild Temptation, and the

113

dire Compulsion of what has once been done...' 'The dire Compulsion of what has once been done'—what a characteristic phrase that is. Clough was always a man to tend his guilt-feelings. He watered them and cossetted them and made them grow. He was like a Chinese restaurant-keeper with his bamboo-shoots. There is nothing really, either in what he has to say of the spasmodic Smith or of Matthew Arnold, to make one think that Clough could ever have been a critic of literature of any consequence. He sees in Arnold—one feels rightly—'a disposition, perhaps, to assign too high a place to what is called Nature', and prefers, as one would expect, the strong and certain 'Morality' to either 'Empedocles' or 'Tristram'.

> But tasks, in hours of insight willed,
> Can be through hours of gloom fulfilled.

Which is Clough's 'Action will furnish belief' without the dubious afterthought. But the article as a whole creaks. The reader has too often the feeling that an undergraduate is at work—a brilliant undergraduate, certainly, but still an undergraduate—sweating and straining after the telling phrase and the rounded, significant paragraph. There is none of 'that happy, unimpeded sequence which' as he himself remarks towards the end of the essay, 'is the charm of really good writers'.

The two 'Letters of Parepidemus' are also over-wrought, but they are none the less much more interesting. The second one is about hexameters, and this is a subject on which Clough of all people is one to be heard. He talks in particular about the business of translating Homer and Virgil into English, and at first sight the conclusions he comes to astonish. Ought they to be done into hexameters, he asks, and roundly answers No. 'It is not an easy thing to make readable English hexameters at all; not an easy thing even in the freedom of original composition, but a very hard one, indeed, amid the restrictions of faithful translation.' And later on he says: 'Homer's rounded line, and Virgil's smooth verse, were both of them...totally unlike those lengthy, straggling, irregular, uncertain slips of *prose mesurée* which we find it so hard to measure, so easy to read in half a dozen ways, without any assurance of the right one, and which, since the days of Voss, the Gothic nations consider analogous to classic hexameter.' Why in God's name, one is tempted immediately to ask, if this is what you think, use hexameters for the *Bothie* and the *Amours*? The answer is to be found by taking together two points already made during discussion of Clough as a writer: Clough was a novelist rather than a poet, and Clough never wrote prose easily; he had to struggle with it, and the sign of his efforts come out on the printed page like sweat upon the brow. He used hexameters, then, because they liberated him somehow from the embarrassments which always tugged at his coat-tails when he was writing prose, and because they were, or at any rate at need could be made, 'anti-poetic', they suited exactly his primarily novelistic purposes. The other letter shows us Clough the revolted Rugbeian, the man who wrote the Uncle's part in the Epilogue to *Dipsychus*. It points to the cardinal deficiencies inherent—perhaps inevitably inherent—in educational systems: 'We submit ourselves for instruction to teachers, and they teach us (or is it our awkwardness that we learn from them?) their faults and mistakes. Each new age and each new year has its new direction; and we go to the well-informed of the season before ours, to be put by them in the direction which, because right for their time, is therefore not quite right for ours.'

Clearly the American solution was not going to be any solution at all. He was worried and wretched, working hard at humdrum, unrewarding tasks and seeing few signs anywhere of a tolerable future for himself. 'I thought yesterday,' he wrote to Blanche on March 24, 'I was really sick of it and that I must positively come back to England without waiting or trying any more...' A tunnel metaphor recurs. He is bewildered and in the dark, but all this is bound to pass. 'Life is very like a railway—one gets into deep-cuttings and long dark tunnels, where one sees nothing, and hears twice as much noise as usual, and one can't read and one shuts up the window and waits and then it all comes clear again.' The Americans were friendly enough. There was Francis Child, a young Harvard don, later to become professor of English, with whom he discussed at one time the possibility of jointly setting up a school, and there was Charles Norton, whose discipleship has already been noted and who, of all the Americans, was the most likely to cause Clough to feel flattered—a quite hypothetical emotional state for him, of course: no man of stature was ever less susceptible to hero-worship than he was. Blanche, in a long and moving letter she wrote to Norton after her husband's death, told him, 'Your friendship has been one of the very great pleasures of his life; indeed he had the truest and warmest affection for you.'

And as well as friendship he got the acclaim due to a successful literary man, though this he could laugh at without any falsity and always, in his letters to Blanche, played down: 'As for poets, "there are four poets in Cambridge" said someone to me the other day—"Mr Longfellow, and you, and Mr Batcheldor, and Mr something else," ' he writes. 'I had, however, to send an autograph to Cincinatti; two hexameter verses, observe.

Written by A. H. Clough, for a reader at Cincinnatti.
Witness his hand and seal this 26th of December.'

—two lines of deliberately atrocious badness, written in self-mockery. Lowell was able to see that his name was not omitted when party invitations were being sent out. 'Afterwards I went to supper to James Lowell, and stayed there from 8.30 to 1 a.m. Thackeray came at ten; Longfellow, Dana, Quincy, Estes Howe, Felton, Fields, and another. Puns chiefly, but Dana is really amusing. Thackeray doesn't sneer; he is really very sentimental; but he sees the silliness sentiment runs into, and so always tempers it by a little banter or ridicule. He is much farther into actual life than I am; I always feel that, but one can't be two things at once you know.'

But in spite of all the genuine friendliness, in spite of the *carrière ouverte aux talents* which he admired in America—'The poor man can get his children educated at the public schools, to which the rich children go also, *for nothing*, prepared for College even'—he could not think of himself as personally making tolerable progress in any direction, let alone the right one. And parties, even with celebrities to listen to, were never very much his line. Religiosity, too, was as vigorously on the rampage at Harvard as in the senior common room at Oriel. 'I...have been getting into a little mysticism lately—perhaps it's all over long ago though, in the last 3 weeks...It won't do, my child. Twice two is four all the world over—and there's no harm in its being so; 'tisn't the devil's doing, that is—il faut s'y soumettre—and all right...Also Charles Norton is too much in the religiose vein to be always quite wholesome company.' By May 1853 he was deeply despondent. 'People...don't know how hard it is for the unfortunate solitary schoolmaster to get through his work from day to day: they don't know how, with no real affection to recur to when he is overworked, he is obliged to run no chances of overworking himself; how he must, as it were, use only his left hand to work with, because he has to *hold on* with his right for fear of falling altogether.' And again later that month: 'I am often desperately sick of country, people, and everything: above all, however, of the climate, which certainly is to my somewhat rheumatic constitution extremely trying during *this* part of [the] year at any rate. Think of passing without notice from 85 degrees in the shade to a cold icy-damp east wind of fifty degrees. This is I believe the real thing that has troubled me so much of late, though partly also it is true that there is a little fatigue of the people.' Once he got out to Shady Hill in early June, his spirits began to rise: 'I woke this morning in a sort of paradise. My room here is a most delightful change from my late narrow crib, consequently I awoke in a sort of ecstasy; I have not been in anything like it since I left Combe.' The change of quarters was not the only reason for this revival. The prospects of a release, of another of those decisive changes of direction which seemed so necessary for him, were becoming less shadowy.

Ever since his sailing for America his friends at home—Carlyle, Lady Ashburton and Frederick Temple in particular—had been looking round for some modest bolt-hole into which their protégé, this balding, brilliant, diffident, would-be married man, might fit. And after the fall of the Derby government in December 1852, the people with places to give became once more responsive to Ashburnham pressure. Earl Granville, Lord President of the Council, felt sure that there ought to be something somewhere for Mr Clough. In the end the matter reduced itself to an either/or—a situation which Clough was never very happy with. The Privy Council secretariat was to be reorganised. Robert Lingen was to be secretary; there were to be two assistant secretaries, and under these six clerks of the first class with salaries of £300 a year rising by £25 a year to £500. One of these clerkships Granville was prepared to offer to Clough. This was the 'either'. It was Frederick Temple himself, the sincerest of well-wishers, who brought in the 'or', and thus unwittingly set up such a dithering as eventually caused tempers to rise on the English side of the Atlantic, if not on Clough's. Temple was Principal of Kneller Hall, a Government Normal School. Palgrave was his Vice-Principal, and Palgrave was eager to have the Council clerkship. Temple, thinking reasonably enough that academic work might well be more congenial to Clough than administrative matters, wrote to him suggesting that if he (Clough) preferred it so, but only (this was stressed) if he preferred it so, Palgrave might offer himself for the reversion of the clerkship and Temple would be glad to welcome him back from America as Vice-Principal of Kneller Hall. Temple wrote urgently to him on May 10 putting all this to him. 'We can do nothing till we get your answer. I believe I have told you everything. And I should be glad of a very speedy reply.'

Temple's letter reached him at the end of May. There were others in the same post, one from Carlyle, enclosing the correspondence between Granville and Lady Ashburton, and there was one from Blanche who enclosed a note from her father in which Samuel Smith made it clear that he could not accept a Council clerkship at £300 a year as a suitable job for any son-in-law of his, and why was he considering the abandonment of his American venture after so brief a trial? So there it was. Should he stick it out in America and hope that his stock would shortly rise? Should he take Temple's £400 a year with board and lodging (but no great prospects) at Kneller Hall? Or should he take the clerkship (which clearly might lead in the long run to a post of considerable responsibility) and hope to soften the not unsusceptible heart of Samuel Smith? He wrote agitatedly to Blanche on May 27. 'I must write 3 or 4 letters before one o'clock and...make up my mind! which heaven only knows how am I to do—Que faire? que faire? que faire?'

In the end he did the typical, disastrous, Cloughian thing: he took no decision at all. He left it to Samuel Smith and Temple. They should decide. He would do whatever seemed best to them. 'I leave the matter entirely in your hands, my dear Sir,' he told Samuel Smith. 'Only I must beg you will not, as I fear you are inclined to do, exaggerate the blessings and the hopes of New England life. I am accustomed myself not to mind little disagreeables, but how far that would be possible in the case of another I don't know...I have a great mind to pack up, and come over by the next steamer to see about the matter, but I shall leave it, I think, for you to decide, *after conferring with Temple*, whom I have empowered to give my answer.'

It is an astonishing letter. Here was a man of thirty-four, a scholar of Balliol, a fellow of Oriel, considered in his own gifted academic circle—and by the rougher, uncloistered genius of Carlyle —as one of the most outstandingly talented men of his generation, asking two men, not to advise—that might have been reasonable enough—but to *decide* in a matter crucially affecting the whole course of his future life. Did he do it out of the deep humility which was always so lovable a part of him? Did he do it because he was tired and dispirited, conscious that his contemporaries, less able, often, than he, were getting ahead while he was lagging, perhaps now irretrievably, behind? Did he do it because above all things he did not want to lose even the distant prospect of Blanche? Whatever the reasons for what he did, the consequences, as was to be expected, were short answers and exasperation. Even Blanche felt obliged to speak out. 'But do not think I cannot bear the waiting, for I know I can. I fear much more the depression effect on you, which I shall always do my best to prevent...The worst fear has been of your losing yourself in inactivity. You see you hardly do anything till you are driven to it by outward pressure—at least you are very apt to wait for that before making up your mind and that *does* make it harder for those who have to deal with you...I may have put it too strongly but is there not a sort of laziness in you, that shrinks from taking the initiative?' Temple was peremptory. 'The conclusion to which Mr Smith has come is: not to decide...And what I have done comes to the same. I have done: nothing. In fact my dear fellow you *cannot* have this matter decided for you...There is nothing left for it but immediate return to England, to choose for yourself.' With this letter from Temple came a second one from Blanche. Anticipating—how grateful he must have been—the duties of a wife, she had made his mind up for him. 'Mr Temple has been here,' she began, 'and I have accepted the Examinership.' 'I sail with this from New York,' he wrote on the same day, 'but this may reach you first— But my views are for America—I hardly know why I should come, but Temple was imperative.' That she too had been imperative does not seem to have occurred to him.

Eight

He was back at Combe Hurst, the Samuel Smiths' house not far from Richmond Park, by the middle of July 1853. People thought he had got fatter. He was thirty-four and a half. He took the eye. The 'golden prime', which Matthew Arnold spoke of, was of course over. The Balliol scholar whom Shairp remembered in a poem long after Clough's death—

> *Foremost one stood, with forehead high and broad—*
> *Sculptor ne'er moulded grander dome of thought—*
> *Beneath it, eyes dark-lustred rolled and glowed,*
> *Deep wells of feeling where the full soul wrought;*
> *Yet lithe of limb, and strong as shepherd boy*

—was by this time quite bald on the top. David Masson, editor of *Macmillan's Magazine* and one of the best-stamina'd of Victorian literary carthorses, thought of the later Clough in these terms: 'A man of very shy demeanour, of largish build about the head and shoulders, with a bland and rather indolent look, and a noticeable want of alertness in his movements.' Crabb Robinson, who was one of the governors of University Hall and who had concurred in his dismissal—'He wants authority and also activity'—still loved him, as who did not? He noted in his diary on October 9: 'Calls from Clough. He is returned from America and has a place in the Education Board...The Yankees were friendly to him and he liked them. He is, however, glad to come back. He looks well and is fatter.' In December there was another visit to record: 'A call from Clough; he was pleasant as man can be. Did not absolutely talk about his intended marriage, but looked it all...'

Were things at last beginning to go right for him? Well, he 'had a place'—one which 'half a hundred people...quite as fit as I am... would give their ears to get.' Samuel Smith had after all relented and decided to help the couple financially so that the lowness of the starting salary in the Privy Council Office need not be a bar to marriage. But he genuinely regretted America. Social inequalities were less glaring there than in England, and less obtrusive. This was something he was grateful for. How different Clough's attitude to America is from the smug self-satisfaction and patronising condescension so painfully noticeable in the American notes of Dickens and Thackeray. 'I like America,' he told Norton immediately on his return, 'all the better for the comparison with England...Certainly I think you are more right than I was willing to admit about the position of the poorer classes here. I hope you will be able to get along without anything like it—and in any case you have a great blessing in the mere chance of that—such is my first *re*-impression.' A reading of the letters he wrote about this time will leave no one in any doubt that he liked the prospect of the Clerkship much less than the prospect of renewing his hand-to-mouth existence in America. But Blanche and her family clearly wanted him to stay in England. Temple too had no doubts about the wisdom of accepting Granville's patronage. Clough, true to the spirit of his last letter from America, 'left it to them to decide'. His docile willingness always to have the collar slipped on to his neck, always to heave away wholeheartedly no matter what lumbering waggon was hitched behind him, was proved once again.

Still, the prospect before him was not unpleasing. He was about to marry very well indeed. And there was, without doubt, deep affection on both sides. Whether there was headlong passion is less certain. It is probable that his rigid upbringing had stunted him so that his passions could never be allowed free flow. At any rate he seems to have uttered no cry of distress at hope deferred when the marriage was arranged to take place a full year ahead. And there were his friends. His friends were glad to see him, glad to know that he was after all to stay amongst them. 'You need not be told,' Carlyle wrote to him on July 22, 'I am delighted at the conclusion you have come to; for my own sake and for yours, I could not wish any other result...May you never repent it: in which case, England and the rest of us will be very far from doing so!' He buckled to, and started work at the Office on Monday morning, July 22. 'I stay in there, up two pair, at the very corner of Downing St and Whitehall, from 11 to 5 or 5½ daily, pretty well occupied all the time.' By the time January, and his thirty-fifth birthday, came round, he was able to tell Norton, 'I live on contentedly enough, but feel rather unwilling to be re-Englished after once attaining the higher transatlantic development—However' (and here he brought in his favourite, and most characteristic, French quotation) 'il faut s'y soumettre, I presume.' He was coming into the administrative grade of the civil service too late in life for there to be any very good chance of reaching the real seats of power; and work in the lower reaches of the top section tended to be, then as now, difficult, responsible and dull. 'Here I am at the desk still,' he wrote to Emerson on September 14, 1855, 'and on the whole preferring the desk to the old task of teaching Greek.' He was able occasionally, even if only in a very small way, to relieve his very genuine political discontent and help toward the slow democratisation of what he once called 'this cruel, unbelieving, inveterate old monarchy'. A boisterous wind from the Crimea blew through Government departmental offices in Whitehall. Clough, up two pair of stairs in Downing Street, did not, of course, get the full force of it. That was withstood, and bull-doggedly withstood, by Lord Panmure the Secretary at War. But still he was able to note with satisfaction, in the letter to Emerson, that some of the comfortable old ways were receiving a jolt: 'We have taken Sevastopol...Our Aristocracy will last now, I suppose, till another great War comes and forces the trading and manufacturing classes to take to fighting. At present our officers come from the gentry and our soldiers mostly from the peasantry or at least the day labourers, much in the old feudal manner. Still I think there has been some change even in this last year—I myself had to help examine about 150 youths, candidates for Commissions in the artillery and engineers—about 40 or 50 of whom were accepted.' In the summer of 1856 he enjoyed another break from routine. It fell to him in the course of duty to act as secretary to a Commission appointed to examine the methods and administration of military schools on the continent. The job took him abroad for three months that summer, visiting Paris, Berlin and Vienna. Vivid, descriptive letters did not come pouring back to England as they had done a few years before from Paris and

Rome; Clough was too busy being the perfect secretary for that. He was hardworking, conscientious, unobtrusive. He was there not to offer opinions but to provide information when information was asked for, and to keep the record. It was a necessary, inglorious role which he accepted with the sweet humility which was always so lovable a part of him. It was also a role which he performed to admiration. Lake, who had been with him at Rugby, was a member of the Commission. He found his services 'invaluable', and there is no reason to suppose that in so saying the future Dean of Durham was indulging in eulogy for old friendship's sake.

He married Blanche Smith at last, on June 13, 1854. He seemed a little uncertain about it right up to the end. 'My *event*,' he told Norton, 'is to take place in all probability about the 15th June.' And then later, 'My *event* is I believe to take place on the 13th June.' 'Another two days from this,' he told Emerson on the 11th, 'will in all probability see me maried.' But in spite of 'I believe' and 'in all probability', married he was, at his wife's home in Derbyshire. Florence Nightingale, strong with the assurance afforded to one who had just won a tough battle for personal independence, came up for her cousin's wedding from her Harley Street 'Institution for the Care of Sick Gentlewomen in Distressed Circumstances'. The eagle may perhaps have cast a meditative eye in Clough's direction, but for the moment was content to let him go. Only four months later, however, on October 21 he was writing to Norton: 'My wife's cousin Florence Nightingale sails tonight for Scutari.' And on the 24th he added to the same letter: 'I went over to Calais on Saturday night to see Florence Nightingale on her way.' The eagle had already begun to crook a masterful finger and beckon.

Children came quickly. The Cloughs moved from Combe Hurst into a home of their own at 11 St Mark's Crescent, Regent's Park, a week after Miss Nightingale's departure for Scutari, and here their first child, a boy who died in infancy, was born in April 1855. Two girls came later, one born in February 1858, and another, Blanche Athena, who was born after he had set out on his last European journey and whom he never saw. She too, like her aunt, Anne Jemima, became Principal of Newnham College and died at a great age. Blanche stresses, in the memoir she wrote as preface to his letters and prose remains, how happy his home life was, how fond he was of children, how he loved playing with them, how his humour, always strong, became now quiet and affectionate and was no longer sarcastic and scorching as in old days. She contemplates with satisfaction the gradual swallowing up of the writer, of the important public figure—this at any rate was how the Americans, Emerson and Lowell in particular, had seen him—in the family man. 'All the new duties and interests of domestic life,' she writes, 'grew up and occupied his daily thoughts...The practical wisdom and insight into life, for which he was distinguished, were constantly exercised in the service of his friends; and the new experience which he was daily gathering at home made many perplexed questions, both social and religous, clear and simple to his mind.'

The letters he wrote at this time go some way towards bearing out this view of him. They are fewer in number than the ones from earlier years. They are written mainly to American friends; they are busy and outward-looking, full of current public events and literary gossip. He detects a small error in Macaulay's *History* and in doing so puts his finger on a central weakness of Macaulay's writing: 'I have only detected one error, myself, but it is a very Macaulayesque one. He speaks of "the oaks of Magdalen"—they are *elms*. There was no occasion to say anything but trees—but the temptation to say something particular was too strong—It makes one distrust all his descriptions.' He still plugged away doggedly at Plutarch, but apart from that seemed almost resentful of any reminder that he was a writer. When, for example, Lowell was bringing out the *Amours* in the *Atlantic Monthly* in 1858, he wrote, almost pettishly, about it to Norton: 'So they have actually printed my hexameters in the *Atlantic*. I cannot myself make up my mind to read them—and it is a great addition to the evil that it will go on for another and another month—I have sent the last portion—which has given me a good deal of trouble. I suppose that what one wrote nine years ago can never be quite agreeable to one—but as I have no time to write now, it was all I could do to send what I had.' He took sedate little holidays during his forty-eight days of annual leave—to Bonn and the Moselle valley in 1855, to a cottage just above Alum Bay in the Isle of Wight in 1856, where he bathed daily, watched the steamers from the Mediterranean and the West Indies pass by on their way to Southampton, and hobnobbed with the Tennysons and the Coventry Patmores. Coventry Patmore's manner of writing interested him, and the effects of that interest are to be seen in the poems of *Mari Magno* which he was shortly to begin working on. He sent prudent driblets of savings across the Atlantic for Norton to invest for him in Massachusetts or Boston stock. He came at last to the end of Plutarch, and Kingsley, always a staunch admirer, wrote to him from Eversley to tell him 'I intend to make my boy use it as a text-book.' In 1861 the *Quarterly* reviewer condescended to it: 'He [Clough] does not the less deserve to have such labours recognised, because they are labours of a kind which would appear exceedingly distasteful to many men (if many such there were) who had given proof so decided as Mr Clough has of original literary genius.' He read travel-books, gave qualified admiration to Tennyson, but thought that 'otherwise England seems as unpoetic as between Chaucer and Spenser.' He met, and liked, young Mr Henry James, and was sorry that his secretarial duties abroad (it was the time of the Commission of Enquiry into military schools on the continent) interrupted a ripening friendship. He occasionally got news of Carlyle, wrestling and groaning in the valley of the shadow of Frederick the Great. He went to Eastbourne for a fortnight 'and there did nothing in the fullest sense of the term. It was a sort of sleep.'

Clearly Blanche's picture of a domestic, untormented, chair-borne-at-the-office Clough is not wholly misleading. It is not an imaginary portrait, painted retrospectively in false colours out of her affectionate concern for what she felt was best for him. There is evidence for it. Nevertheless it is a picture which, consciously or otherwise, leaves a great deal out. Did religion matter, or was it something small enough to justify a sleepy, offhand conformity? The question worried him as much as ever. He wrote to William Allingham, the poet and journalist, in January 1856: 'I watched out the old year rather sleepily at a family party; where people sang and acted charades. I find myself recoil as yet from any Church or Chapel and even from the family prayers into which circumstances sometimes hurry one. I could almost believe it to be one's duty to take up one's parable and protest or at any rate to take oneself off. Yet I hesitate—and probably, but for the pressure of circumambient dogmatism and conformity, should not feel the impulse.' Another question arises as we contemplate this 'happy and peaceful though laborious life' described by Blanche. Why should it have been so laborious? Eleven till five, and forty-eight days leave a year—there have been civil servants who have contrived a quite massive literary output under conditions similar to these. Anthony Trollope's job in the Post Office was as responsible as Clough's and probably more time-consuming, yet he managed to make £70,000 out of novel-writing. Matthew Arnold, as Inspector of Schools, was certainly as fully occupied as Clough—and lamented the claims of his official life much more copiously than Clough ever did—yet there he was, by 1858, a fully arrived literary figure of the first magnitude, and Professor of Poetry at Oxford into the bargain, receiving about £100 a year for four lectures, and freezing the literate public with the marmoreal chill of *Merope*. In a way, of course, Clough's honest pleasure in the success of his friends, the sincerity of his disinclination to keep up with people, is one of the pleasantest things about him. 'Though without much fame,' as Bagehot said, 'he had no envy.' Yet surely there ought to have been time for at least some original writing, time for something better than compiling the index to Plutarch? 'He had not time or strength or leisure of mind,' says Blanche, 'to spend on his natural gift of writing; and to his friends it must ever be a source of sorrow that his natural vocation, what he himself felt as such, was unfulfilled.' Why had he no time? Blanche knew the answer to this question perfectly well.

The answer was Florence Nightingale. 'But the work,' says Blanche, 'in which he took the deepest interest was that of his friend and relation, Miss Nightingale. He watched over every step in her various undertakings, affording her assistance not merely with advice, and little in his life gave him greater satisfaction than to be her active and trusted friend.' These prim and blameless sentences, concealing what must have been a deep resentment on Blanche's part, are all she offers towards the unfolding of one of the strangest of stories.

The story starts with that sentence of Clough already quoted—'I went over to Calais on Saturday night to see Florence Nightingale on her way' (to Scutari). It ends with that astonishing outburst which Florence Nightingale wrote to Madame Mohl on December 13, 1861, exactly one month after Clough's death: 'A woman once told me my character would be more sympathised with by men than by women. In one sense I don't choose to have that said. Sidney Herbert and I were together exactly like two men—exactly like him and Gladstone. And as for Clough, oh Jonathan, my

brother Jonathan, my love for thee was very great, PASSING THE
LOVE OF WOMEN...People often say to me, you don't know what a
wife and mother feels. No, I say, I don't and I'm very glad I don't
And *they* don't know what *I feel*. Why, dear soul, Blanche went
away and left her husband for a year! I am the only person who
made any effort to save his life and gave him £500 to go abroad,
my hard earned savings. And they are living on that now, his wife
and sisters, at Florence...Ezekiel went running about naked, "for
a sign". I can't run about naked because it is not the custom of the
country. But I would mount three widows' caps on my head, "for
a sign". And I would cry. This is for Sidney Herbert, I am his real
widow. This is for Arthur Clough, I am his true widow (and I
don't find it a comfort that I had two legs to cut off, whereas other
people have but one). And this, the biggest widow's cap of all, is
for the loss of all sympathy on the part of my nearest and dearest...'
     At either end of Clough's life there stood a devouring, demand-
ing person. At the outset, it was Thomas Arnold. Under those
flashing eyes, that rallying, sermonising tongue, the biddable,
clever, indolent little boy from South Carolina turned himself into
a model of strenuous, evangelical piety. He did good with a
neurotic single-mindedness which left him warped and listless for
a decade. At the close came Florence Nightingale, a stronger
character even than Arnold, more unscrupulous, more domineering, a daimonic boa-constrictor of a woman who swallowed
cabinet ministers whole and who seized upon talented good-will
wherever she found it and drove it to self-destruction. Clough's
responsiveness to her was total. His relationship to her brings out
better than anything else in his life his complicated, contradictory
nature. Intellectually he was powerful, stubborn and independent.
Emotionally, temperamentally, he always looked for a lead.
Without himself being fully aware of it, he longed always for
dedication. The snugness of enlistment, of being under orders,
was something greatly desirable, yet something which his intelligence kept shifting outside his reach. As he made Claude say in
Amours de Voyage:

> *Great is Fate, and is best. I believe in Providence partly.*
> *What is ordained is right, and all that happens is ordered.*
> *Ah, no, that isn't it. But yet I retain my conclusion.*
> *I will go where I am led, and will not dictate to the chances.*

'Fluctuate' was Matthew Arnold's word for it. 'You are too content to fluctuate', he told him in a letter written six months before his marriage. Matthew Arnold did not always understand him, but he comes very close here to the essential Clough, and certainly no two English poets were ever closer than these two, especially in the crucial years of their middle twenties.

Clough kept a close watch on Florence Nightingale's famous doings at Scutari. 'Here,' he wrote to Emerson on May 7, 1855, 'we are meanwhile publicly, as it seems to me, better for being at war; and for not being altogether as successful as we thought we should be. I hear occasionally of Florence Nightingale's proceedings at Scutari, where she is doing pretty hard work—controlling nurses and contending with doctors and officials.—She is my wife's first cousin by the father's and the mother's side; and I, as it happened, had the honour of being her escort as far as Calais. You know, I dare say, that Milnes was for a long time her suitor...'

When, in May 1855, she fell ill he was filled with anxiety—by this time, it should be said, in company with the majority of his fellow-countrymen. 'This Crimean fever is a dreadful sickness—she describes herself as suffering "from a compound fracture of the intellects".' She recovered sufficiently to make the journey back from Balaclava, not to England but to Scutari, and thence, after a short convalescence, to return to the Crimea for a renewal of her struggle with Dr John Hall, Chief of Medical Staff of the British Expeditionary Army, who, as she said, 'would like to broil her slowly on the fires of her own diet kitchen'.

In August 1856 she was back in England. The Crimean War had been won. She was a national heroine. But she looked on all this not as a climax, a fulfilment, but as a beginning. Crimea for her represented not victory but calamity. Seventy-three men out of every hundred had died there in six months—not from wounds but from diseases which a properly organised medical service could have prevented. Reform would have to come and it would have to be drastic and far-reaching. And reform would have to come through her, a weak woman, and through her alone. For the politicians the Crimean War had been an unfortunate business, a regrettable incident which was best forgotten. She would have to needle them, jab them, jolt them, drive them. And she would have to do it now, while the ghastly business was still vivid in people's minds and while she herself still stood clear and sympathetic in the public imagination—the personification of womanly tenderness and devotion. 'I stand,' she wrote that August, 'at the altar of the murdered men, and while I live I fight their cause.' To do this she had to find fresh gifts within herself. It was not her genius for nursing that was needed now, not even primarily her astounding administrative flair. She had to become a lobbying familiar, a committee-woman, an indefatigable writer of minutes, a tireless winkler-out of entrenched officials, a setter-out-at-length of incontrovertible facts. She had to seek out her enemies and destroy them. But these enemies were men, with clubs to retire to and well-defended Whitehall offices to lurk in. She was a mid-Victorian woman whose place was the boudoir. She wanted to get at Lord Panmure, the Secretary-at-War, but it was August after all and he was grouse-shooting in Scotland. And how could she jump the purdah-walls of her boudoir and chase him up the bens? She needed a man, men even. A war could not be conducted from a base-camp; she would have to have officers and men to carry out her orders in the field. There was Sidney Herbert. He was sympathetic. He had officer-like qualities. He could tackle the Panmures in their secret places. And there was Clough. Had he officer-like qualities? She wasn't sure, but at any rate he was intelligent and he was willing. He would be invaluable when it came to the paper-work.

Clough was with her that August, acting as secretary and messenger. Gradually her demands upon his time increased. Her *Notes on Matters affecting the Health, Efficiency and Hospital Administration of the British Army*—the work which was to supply the ammunition for the Royal Commission of Enquiry—ran to a thousand closely printed pages. By the summer of 1857, when Lord Panmure, yielding finally to a combination of blandishments, threats and persistence, agreed to set up the Commission, Clough was working long hours with her, or for her. Letters flew between the office at the corner of Downing Street and Whitehall and the Burlington Hotel, her London headquarters. 'I send by Post,' he wrote on September 6, 1857, '(if the Post does not refuse it) the Diagrams—also the last sheet, pp. 240 to 256—and the first new sheet of this revise—those in a separate packet. The Diagrams were in Burlington St. with various letters, which I will get *revised* at Combe tomorrow and forward or leave accordingly—The Printers cannot get on very fast with this work, as one man must do it all they say…My work here is I am glad to say beginning to relax a little. So if you have any more commissions—pray consider me.' She had plenty more commissions. On September 28 he was writing: 'I enclose 2D.—2E has come and shall be sent tomorrow—a letter and a card are enclosed—a package from the Admiralty —Medical and Statistical Returns of Baltic and Black Sea Fleets during 54, 55 has also come. Do you want it?…Lord Panmure is still on the moors.' Two days later he was writing again: 'Yesterday I sent 2E. Today I have from you 2A, 2B, 2C, 2D—I hope to send 2F (if not 2G): also a copy of the whole from K to 2E inclusive.' Four months later it was still the same story. 'I send today a mass of précis. What is in the bag I have examined—the other package I send for your trouble, in order not to delay. This is what I am to go through after—is it not.' And the very next day: 'I send some more précis—which I think must be the end of it.—I have put in a few alterations and additions in the Defects and Suggestions—*some* of which seem to be wanted. We had a bad account of you this morning, but you were said to be mending at 3 p.m. yesterday.' By this time, as the last sentence of Clough's note shows, Miss Nightingale had relapsed into her fifty years of invalidism—an invalidism which in 1858 was part tactical, part genuine and brought on by stupendous overwork.

But the stupendous overwork was shared; she saw to that. Sidney Herbert toiled at high policy level. Clough toiled over the details. He was courier as well as secretary. 'I have ordered your Coach and your Carriage for Monday,' he wrote to her on February 5, 1858. 'There is no apparent reason to expect the event in our household just yet—The Nurse however will come tomorrow. If all remains as it is, I should wish to start on Sunday at 2 p.m., sleep at Malvern and return with you the next day.' This was when Blanche was expecting her second baby, who was born five days later on the 10th. 'Blanche would wish it to be so,' Clough went on reassuringly in case Miss Nightingale should have any misgivings about taking off her cousin's husband at such a moment. But one wonders perhaps how much insistence Blanche managed to put into these wishes of hers.

After the baby was born Blanche went off to the family home at Combe Hurst, leaving her husband to stay on alone at 11 St Marks' Terrace during the week. There are no indications anywhere of an estrangement, but partial separation it certainly was.

The labouring went on. On August 9 he wrote to Miss Night-ingale: 'I send something from the printer and will send more tomorrow—I believe the Saty Review will be disposed to accept an article. But I think the Article you have written requires a good deal of alteration as well as abridgement. When I have made my suggested changes I shall send it to you. I have ordered the two blue books for your Doctors, and the *North British* will reach you I hope by tomorrow's post.' On the 20th: 'End of Appendix to XIV—received and sent to press. Letter to Mr Bellamy received and forwarded. SR Article returned—received this morning and will be attended to.' On the 26th: 'The *draft* for Harrisons [the printers]—and the return Preface came to St Mark's this morning: also the "fag end of the Nurses," last night—also, the order for the samples of covers, yesterday morning...I have gone through *all* the figures...I have seen the Stove at Soyers and hope to get it off tomorrow by goods train.' She drove him hard. 'Clough,' she wrote, with the megalomania common to all those who grapple successfully with human inertia, 'a poet born if ever there was one, takes to nursing administration...for me.' He was content to do it, content, as she put it on another occasion, 'to do the work of a cabhorse'.

The strain of fulfilling the demands of two exacting taskmasters —the Education Committee of the Privy Council on the one hand and the frail, febrile dynamo reclining on her couch at the Burling-ton Hotel on the other—began to tell on him. Symptoms of exhaustion appeared, like those he had suffered at the climax of his career at Rugby after winning the Balliol scholarship. But now he was forty and not as resilient as he had been in that December twenty-three years earlier when he had sat in Arnold's drawing-room being fussed over by Mrs Arnold and writing to Simpkinson about his doings at Balliol. In December 1859 he caught what was diagnosed as 'scarletina'. It was an inopportune moment for an infectious illness. A removal from 11 St Mark's Terrace to Campden Hill, Kensington, a house 'just below Maculay's', had recently been carried out, and a little boy was born to them on the 16th. He wrote to Norton on December 29: 'I have been sent here for ventilation, after an attack of scarletina, which made me an inconvenient neighbour to a little boy just born to us.' The place chosen for his 'ventilation' was Hastings, but the weather was rainy and stormy, and, although he returned to his desk on

January 10, he was slow to recover. It was from the time of this attack that Blanche noted in him 'a gradual going down hill'. The following summer he broke his toe. 'No fair reason against using one's fingers,' he said, 'but it prevents one's walking, and impairs one's energies in general.' An autumn holiday in Scotland, where they stayed with Sir John MacNeill, a Crimean Commissioner and another satellite in the Nightingale solar system, failed to restore him to full energy. Before Christmas his doctor told him to take six months' rest, and, to begin with, sent him to Malvern for five weeks for the water cure—a shudderingly rigorous process involving the wrapping of nakedness in cold, wet sheets. He was at Campden Hill Road for Christmas and then returned to submit to more punishment at Malvern for a second five weeks. After that they went to Freshwater Bay in the Isle of Wight, where they had been before. 'My husband is better, thank you,' Blanche wrote to Miss Norton on March 10, 1861, 'though I cannot feel very easy about him yet. It is not a dangerous state of health *unless* he overworks himself again, but in our position it is so hard for him to avoid that that it makes our future very uncertain...We have now been here nearly a fortnight and he is better, but he has been suffering so much from rheumatism and neuralgia that he has not had much power of feeling it.' The Tennysons were kind neighbours, and the two Tennyson boys of seven and nine patronised the three-year-old Florence 'to her heart's content'.

Freshwater did him good. Blanche cherished the memory of those days. It was the last time—and perhaps, in the fullest sense, the first time also—that he enjoyed family life with his children. He carried them on his back down country lanes, listened to Florence learning to talk, rose early for a pre-breakfast walk across the downs, and began, very tentatively, to write again. The doctors, however, were still not satisfied. They thought that, without another change of air and perhaps some foreign travel, he would not be able to hold his gains. And so, in the middle of April 1861, with Miss Nightingale's £500—'my hard-earned savings'— he set off, alone, for Greece and Constantinople.

Nine

TRAVEL always released his creativeness. Once alone and abroad, the trickle which had begun to flow in Freshwater broadened to a full stream. The first, and probably most of the second stories of the series called *Mari Magno* were written during the course of the Greek journey which lasted until about June 24, and he was writing hard at these stories till his death seven months later. He was his own man briefly once again, not being driven by the demands of Florence Nightingale or of the office, not being stiflingly mothered by Blanche. (Jowett thought that his marriage 'was the real blessing and happiness of his life', but what Jowett knew wasn't always knowledge.) There is certainly a sense in which Blanche Smith was good for him. She was someone to run to, someone behind whose skirts his psychological disarray could hide. She was a consolation for the defeated part of him. But her influence on him as a creative writer was dire. And there are signs, all through the long courtship and brief marriage, that Clough was perfectly well aware of this. There is always a latent, unexpressed uneasiness in their relationship, a suppressed hankering on his part after the creative work which he knew deep inside him, if only he could get away, he was capable of.

Mari Magno is like nothing else he wrote. Here there are no dialogues with himself. He looks outward. The novelist in him begins in real earnest to get the upper hand. The work is a collection of stories in verse. Like Boccaccio, Chaucer, and other (infinitely more skilled) storytellers before him, he has to find a framework. He thinks back to that voyage out to New England on the *Canada*. Travellers making their way across oceans need pastimes. Why not collect a few together and have them tell each other stories? The group is quite small: himself ('a youth was I'), an elder friend (thirty-three and a rising lawyer), an English clergyman, fifty years old,

> *...he had not known*
> *The things pertaining to his cloth alone...*
> *Serious and calm, yet lurked, I know not why,*
> *Sometimes a softness in his voice and eye.*
> *Some shade of ill a prosperous life had crossed;*
> *Married no doubt; a wife a child had lost?*

And one, 'of the New England ancient blood...His youthful spurs in letters he had won', was undoubtedly modelled on Lowell. It is this one, whom they call New England or the Pilgrim Son, who suggests the tale-telling and proposes further that they shall be 'of love and marriage' the lawyer begins, the first evening out, with a tale called 'Primitiae', or 'Third Cousins'.

The first paragraph leaves you a bit flabbergasted.

> *Dearest of boys, please come today,*
> *Papa and Mama have bid me say,*
> *They hope you'll dine with us at three;*
> *They will be out till then, you see,*
> *But you will start at once, you know,*
> *And come as fast as you can go.*
> *Next week they hope you'll come and stay*
> *Some time, before you go away.*
> *Dear boy, how pleasant it will be!*
> *Ever your dearest Emily!*

Is the man falling into premature dotage?

He isn't of course. The opening paragraph is a letter written by a fourteen-year-old girl. Clough is trying to catch the prattle and the innocence, and is conscious too, perhaps, of Coventry Patmore's manner in 'The Angel in the House'—'The Angel in the House of Coventry Patmore has some merit I think,' he had told Norton in January 1855, and Emerson wrote to him from Concord in March 1856 to say, 'We read good books from your country, and last, "The Angel in the House". Several of your friends believe, in spite of contradiction, that the poem is yours.' Perhaps the 'Lawyer's First Tale' can be thought of as Clough's reply to this

134

remark of Emerson's. It tells of adolescent love, of the student-intellectual who wants Emily, one of a country clergyman's bevy of daughters, but is clumsy and awkward in his approaches. The lawyer talks ruefully of the boy he was:

> *I own it was the want, in part,*
> *Of any teaching of the heart.*
> *It was, now hard at work again,*
> *The busy argufying brain*
> *Of the prize schoolboy...*

He loses her of course, to a sprightly young landowner called Helston, meets the couple holidaying in Switzerland—the confrontation is beautifully done—and visits them again back home. She asks him about his University triumphs and his future. He 'very likely might stay on', he tells her, 'And lapse into a college don.' But Emily advises against—college and school were only play—'Sometime you'll wish to have a wife.' He reacts strongly. 'You speak,' he tells her,

> *'Just as if any wife would do*
> *...Emilia, when I've heard,' I said,*
> *'How people match themselves and wed,*
> *I've sometimes wished that both were dead.'*

She tells him not to be so vehement, that he has a great future, but

> *It does not matter much,' said I,*
> *'The things I thought of are gone by:*
> *I'm quite content to wait and die.'*

And a little further on

> *'O Emily, was it ever told,'*
> *I asked, 'that souls are young and old?'*

'The Clergyman's First Tale' follows. This is in heroic couplets —or unheroic couplets might perhaps be a better description because they are muted, down-to-earth and have a certain Crabbe-like air about them. It describes a young man's hesitations before committing himself to marriage. 'Action will furnish belief—but will that belief be the true one?'—The question that eternally nagged at Clough is here exteriorised in action:

135

>   *'Would I could wish my wishes all to rest,*
>   *And know to wish the wish that were the best!'*

'The American's Tale' is an anecdote wordy and quite without value. (It must be remembered always when thinking about *Mari Magno* that Clough was writing at speed and didn't live long enough to revise and select. Had he come back to it, this illustration of the theme of love by accident—he calls it 'Juxtaposition'— would have been rejected.)

'My Tale' is a travelogue based upon his recently completed journey in the Auvergne and the Pyrenees. The central theme of the poems—love and marriage—is rather lost sight of here. It is impressionistic, not very closely knit together and can be thought of, made up as it is of small contributions made by coach-travellers winding their way through the hills of Auvergne, as a reproduction-in-miniature of the pattern of *Mari Magno* as a whole. It praises country simplicity at the expense of urban sophistication, and in it Clough seems to be harking back to the mood out of which came the refrain of 'Les Vaches' written in London, probably, in November 1849:

>   *'Home, Rose, and home, Provence and La Palie.'*

He was always good at refrains. The best one here comes in the song sung by the conductor of the *diligence*, as the heavy coach lumbers, crowded with passengers westwards from La Quenille to Tulle in the Auvergne.

>   *'Adieu, gay loves, it is too late a day.'*

Next the *Canada's* Mate tells a not very memorable little anecdote of a mid-nineteenth century *au pair* girl, stranded in Liverpool on her way back to Bordeaux, with a month to wait for the next boat and no money for bed and board, who finds her predicament solved by an offer of marriage (genuine, non-bigamous) from the captain of the tramp steamer who has brought her over from her post in Ireland.

'The Clergyman's Second Tale' is about adultery, and Clough's line is that too much—the Victorian too much—must not be made of it. A man, separated from loving wife and family for a long stretch whilst he convalesces abroad from an illness, may easily and forgivably forget himself in a chance encounter with a pretty

136

woman ('Juxtaposition in short, and what is juxtaposition?'). An elaborate rigmarole of remorse is out of place. And it is his wife who hammers home the point when at last he comes back to her:

> *'And after all, you know we are but dust,*
> *What are we, in ourselves that we should trust?'*

In 'The Lawyer's Second Tale' Clough returns to the Highland background of *The Bothie*. The gentlemanly young man seduces the innocent illiterate Highland lass, means to marry, hesitates too long over the unsuitability of it, and loses her: she has sailed for Australia with her aunt and uncle, Macfarlane the Grocer. Years later they meet again, both married, she now prosperous as he is—and literate even—and their son is a tall young man. She tells him how she consoled herself long ago on that long voyage out:

> *'Ah, well, I said, but now at least he's free,*
> *He will not have to lower himself for me,*
> *He will not lose three hundred pounds a year,*
> *In many ways my love has cost him dear.'*

The flat couplets artfully underline the triteness and hollowness of the 'morality' Clough is satirising. Class distinctions, inimatable, heaven-sent according to mid-Victorian ideas, are quietly mocked and given a gentle shaking. They go aboard ship—he is taking her from the Highlands to Glasgow and the Grocer—and

> *Around the Mull the passage now to make*
> *They go aboard and separate tickets take,*
> *First-class for him, and second-class for her.*

The tale is demurely devastating in the same way as, speaking in his own voice, Clough had been in 'The Latest Decalogue'.

The stories in *Mari Magno* have prompted many questions. Are they simply the infantile scribblings of a once talented man knowing now that he is gripped by terminal illness yet pressing on, much too rapidly, knowing that he is a writer and knowing that there are fresh forms to be hammered out for what he wants to say, for what obsesses him? Was Henry Sidgwick right when he called the poem 'the genius of twaddle'? Is it, as someone much later said, 'the most embarrassingly dreadful long poem of the nineteenth century'? Or was Blanche right when she said that what he

137

wanted was 'to create a new treatment of old subjects, to turn them over and bring them out in the new light of his critical but kindly philosophy'? Was James Addington Symonds right when he spoke out more strongly than did even his widow: *Mari Magno* was 'the ripest product of his mind' and with it he gained 'a place among the poets of the world'?

Any attempt at answering these questions must begin by firmly tackling Henry Sidgwick. His 'genius of twaddle' serves only to demonstrate how completely a sapient man can fail to see what a poet is up to. Clough was aiming at a poetry of social commentary, with a strong story line in the manner of Crabbe. And Coventry Patmore, who interested him, had suggested some fresh ideas on style. He wanted to be plain, to get character into his dialogue as a novelist does. He wanted to avoid 'high sentence'. He wanted to achieve a manner that was fluent and relaxed, catching the flavour of Victorian after-dinner conversation, yet salting it with irony.

As a poet Clough is always a man in a hurry. The stuff has to come quickly or not at all. On the whole I would prefer to call this a characteristic and not a fault. It is something he shares with Byron. But there can be no doubt that in *Mari Magno* the urge to press on does sometimes become altogether too imperative. He is like an aeroplane flying dangerously low. '*Il rase la prose*', as the French describe Racine's technique of verse-writing. And some-times he dips into disaster. Still, his intentions are reasonable and worthwhile—and, more often than not, realised.

> We made a party in a boat,
> And rowed to Sea-Mew island out,
> And landed there and roved about:
> And I and Emily out of reach
> Strayed from the rest along the beach.
> Looking into a sort of cave
> She stood, when suddenly a wave
> Ran up; I caught her by the frock,
> And pulled her in, and o'er a rock,
> So doing, stumbled, rolled, and fell.
> She knelt down, I remember well,
> Bid me where I was hurt to tell,
> And kissed me three times as I lay;
> But I jumped up and limped away.

138

A sexual exchange between a twelve-year-old and a fourteen-year-old would be handled differently today, but Clough conveys the truth of the matter with confident sureness.

He reached Athens by April 24. 'I'm two pairs up, looking towards the Acropolis,' he told Blanche. He found it a very pleasant place to stay at 'in the lounging way'. Not that he seems to have lounged very much. His letters home, carefully impersonal, are full of bustle and activity. The weather was fine, but with a fresh breeze blowing and the land green still with young barley. He walked hard, rode a horse with a Greek saddle—'the most dreadful invention in the world'—and by Easter Sunday (May 5, Orthodox style) was 'tired and a little out of sorts at night, and so did not sit up to see the hullabaloo at 12 p.m., when the king and queen, after attending divine service, come out upon a platform and show themselves, in honour of the great event, and in token that ὁ Χριστὸς ἀνέστη'. On the 17th, he left the Piraeus by steamer for Constantinople. Here, still a strenuous tourist in by now changeable weather, he stayed in a hotel that was 'costly, but comfortable in its way, if one only had not to stay in it altogether'. He saw the Sultan going to Mosque in his twenty-oared caique, who looked, he thought, 'quite "the sick man of Europe". When he got on shore, a sort of chant was set up, interpreted to us as "O Sultan! Trust not in yourself; there is God above, who is greater than you", which was not saying very much.' At this point Clough detached himself from his companions, and went back to the hotel, 'and then over to Scutari with Dr Pincoff, and saw all Scutari, Barrack and General Hospitals, and F.N.'s own tower, and rooms, and everything.' It was territory which, in one sense, he already knew backwards. On June 24, after two months away, he returned to London.

There is a certain lack of zest in the accounts he sent home of this first tour. All the sights are dutifully seen; the cistus and thyme are in blossom at Phyle; Euboea and Marathon lie as on a map below him as he stands on the arbutus-clad slopes of Pentelicus, but somehow he fails to thrill to it in the way one would expect of perhaps the finest classical scholar of his generation. 'I have got back a little tired, but no worse.' That is the sort of summing-up he tends to give at the end of an excursion. The doctors shook their heads. The wine-dark seas had not refreshed him. He must set out on further travels. He wrote to Emerson on July 4, not from home, but from Miss Nightingale's headquarters at the Burlington, 'This London life has been rather too hard for me—though I have not gone into the hot fire of Society—in November I shall try and tackle it again in one way or other.'

The next day he left England for the last time. He crossed to Dieppe—'without disagreeables though there was some sea'—slept there, and came on to Paris the next day where he stayed in the Rue du Bac with the Mohls. (Madame Mohl was Miss Nightingale's 'Clarkey', tiny, fascinating, despiser of women, presider over the most brilliant *salon* of nineteenth-century Paris, friend of Chateaubriand and Guizot.) There had been talk, whilst he was back in England, of yet another change of job. His Privy Council secretaryship was at once strenuous and sedentary. Might it not be possible to find something which did not involve quite so much daily hurrying office routine? Sir Harry Verney, who had married Miss Nightingale's sister, Parthenope, thought perhaps something might be managed if Palmerston were spoken to. Shairp wrote from Edinburgh to say that a Scotch Professorship might suit him very well—'no subscription, except a general statement that you will not try to overthrow the Established Church.' Letters full of these plans followed him abroad, but he could summon up no enthusiasm. 'It was quite a relief to learn that nothing was actually pressing and no necessity urging, for immediate decision.'

From Paris he went to the Auvergne—to Mont Dore les Bains. The last part of the journey was done by diligence, a stiff forty-four kilometres out of the valley of the Allier over the Puy de Dome range and down into the valley of the Gironde. They took seven and a quarter hours, 'and I, dare say, walked for 1½ hours uphill.' There was life in him yet. But he was lonely. The hotel was full; the French, solidly trustful of spa-cures then as now, were there in strength. There were fifty for *déjeuner* at ten and fifty again for dinner at half past five. And, so it was very comforting indeed to run across the Tennysons early one morning as he was crossing the *place* on his way to the café. Tennyson was in flight from Freshwater. The summer holiday season was beginning, and the cockneys had been trooping down to the Isle of Wight and peeping over hedges to get a glimpse of him. Clough showed them round, took young Hallam on horseback, ride and tie, to the waterfall at Quéreult, and agreed readily to change his plans and follow them down to Luchon in the Pyrenees as soon as his boots came back from the cobbler's.

Blanche was urging him to apply for a further extension of his leave, but the loneliness, even with the prospect of Pyrenees-scramblings with Tennyson ahead, made him mutinous, although ultimately, as always, his docility triumphed. 'I don't want at all to spend a winter abroad, away from the children...I think I will wait till I hear from you again...before sending any letter of application. I don't understand why I am all of a sudden to apply, nor what you are thinking about doing. I hope however you will keep quiet and not bother yourself—that is *your* FIRST DUTY at present.' (Blanche was expecting another baby.) Blanche sent him a long, scolding answer. The return home at the end of June had been a mistake—'I am sure...the time and the associations and return to old thoughts were very bad for you—and if you return you cannot be certain of not running those risks and being dragged into what you don't foresee...You do not know how much grief it gave me to feel sure you had done yourself harm this time, and all through these months since your health failed I have had the feeling that you *would* not look forward, that you would only plan when the decision was so imminent as to be too late. *Quem Deus vult perdere prius dementat.* Sometimes I have been afraid the first process has begun...' And so, obediently, on July 28 from Tarbes, he sent his application to the Secretary of the Education Department of the Privy Council. 'If on the 18th of February I find I am still unable to resume my work I shall ask you to place my resignation in the Lord President's hands.' He was still peevish at having done as he had been told when he reached Luchon on the 30th. 'No Tennyson discoverable yet. I think it very funny of you people at home—Flo and all of you—to suppose that it can be so very pleasant or easily endurable to stay poking about abroad for more than two or three months at a time, all by oneself or something no better—or perhaps worse.'

Luchon was hot and crowded, a sort of mountain Brighton. In a few days he got word that the Tennysons were, after all, at Bigorre, and he was glad to have the prospect of joining them—'for it is rather solitary work going about Pyreneeing with a horse and guide.' Important news from home reached him too. Sidney Herbert, the right hand of the man-eating Miss Nightingale as

Clough had been the left, died on August 2, and an exhaustion similar to Clough's seems to have been the cause of it. On the 5th Blanche gave birth to a daughter. 'I think you must call her *Blanche Athena*,' he wrote, 'but if you don't like it, I won't insist.' He wandered restlessly about from Luchon to Pierrefitte, from Pierrefitte to Luz-St Sauveur, thence back to Luchon again and then, at the beginning of September, to Cauterets where he and Tennyson walked together and Tennyson growlingly remembered the holiday he had taken in the same place thirty-one years before with Hallam. Here, looking at the peaks that climbed high all round, he spoke of how he had been moved to write 'Oenone'. Clough, still busy with the series of verse-tales he had begun on the journey to Greece and Constantinople, sent occasional snippets home, kept strenuously 'Pyreneeing about' by horse and diligence in spite of the great heat, and waited for the time when Blanche would be strong enough to come out and join him. 'As for your coming out...I entreat you not to start too soon; the fatigues of crossing France by railway are considerable, and to fatigue yourself after starting would be a greater delay than waiting...Subject to your finding some escort I should prefer your waiting till October 2—the earliest date at which you can bring my salary warrant...I would then come to Dieppe or Boulogne or indeed Newhaven or Folkstone just to take you: and we would go off to Geneva via Dijon and to the Simplon.' But Blanche jumped the gun. She left London on September 17 and was in Paris, at the Hotel des Deux Mondes, on the 18th. He hurried northwards to join her.

To Blanche when she saw him then, he seemed nervous but not seriously unwell. He could hardly bear hearing about the children whom he had not been allowed to revisit. The Tennysons said good-bye to him with the utmost affection and regret. Tennyson had listened while he read the parts of *Mari Magno* already completed and had shared the author's strong emotion. Mrs Tennyson had seen much of the sweet serviceableness which was always so strong in him. 'We had a sad parting from Mr Clough at Pau,' she wrote. 'There could not have been a gentler, kinder, more unselfish or more thoughtful companion than he has been. Among other things he corrected the boys' little journals for them.' —Can one imagine the author of 'Oenone' ever bending so low?— 'We called him "the child-angel".' He was irked too at Blanche's having come a fortnight before he had planned. He had been looking forward to coming as far as the south coast of England to fetch her. It would have been good to have seen England once again, and 'if' (I came) 'to Folkestone or Newhaven you might perhaps bring Florence just to see me.'

But there it was. Blanche was in Paris. The three little children were far away at Combe Hurst in England, and Blanche Athena he was never to see. They stayed two or three days in Paris, and then went south-east to Dijon and Salins, thence by diligence to Pontarlier, then over the Simplon in heavy snow and down to Stresa. At Stresa he was feverish, and instead of staying a while and moving on to Como as they had intended, they went straight through to Milan. There he rallied. They made excursions. At Parma he took great delight in the Correggios. 'He enjoyed the Correggios excessively,' Blanche wrote to Norton. 'You will perhaps be shocked at this, but he did, and you know when he enjoyed anything, there was a perfection about his pleasure which made it perfectly delightful to see.' After that came fitful neuralgic pains of great intensity. Blanche was anxious by this time to reach as quickly as possible a doctor she felt she could trust. And so they embarked on two days' *vetturino* over the Apennines, down through the olives and chestnuts to Pistoia, and at length to Florence, where Miss Nightingale had been born forty-one years earlier, and where he was to die five weeks later.

The doctor—a 'good and kind' one, Dr Wilson—diagnosed low malarial fever, and he helped Blanche to find him a lodging away from the hotel. Gradually the feverish attacks subsided, and, immediately and busily, he went to his writing. After a fortnight —on the 24th—things seemed much brighter again. He was working hard indoors, revising, in feeble pencil, the tales already written for *Mari Magno*, and writing, or dictating, new ones. But then, round about November 1, there came a relapse. Signs of paralysis appeared in a leg and an eye. He ceased to be able to fix his thoughts, and occasionally he wandered. It began to look as though he was nearing his end. Anne was sent for and reached Florence on the 10th. On the evening of the 13th the doctor visited him at eight and thought him no worse. Blanche left his bedside at ten to lie down, leaving Anne with him. About a quarter to eleven Anne came for her. He seemed to be growing cold, she said. For a long time the two women sat there, watching the quiet, losing struggle. Then suddenly he spoke up quite strongly, asking for some water. Blanche gave him some seltzer, and he said, 'Who is that? Blanchy?' She said 'Yes', and bent over him. He kissed her, and then he kissed Anne. 'Do you send your love to the children?' Blanche asked him. And he answered, strongly still, 'Yes, dear. I always send my love to the children.' He said no more after that, and a little later, at one in the morning, he set out on the last journey of all.

Post-Mortem

I REMEMBER a schoolmaster of mine who used to enforce a good rule. Each week he made us learn some English poetry off by heart. One week he took the sad and stately stanzas from *Thyrsis* that have already sounded murmurously through these pages:

> *Too quick despairer, wherefore wilt thou go?*
> *Soon will the high midsummer pomps come on...*

and I asked this imposer of important tasks: 'Who *was* this despairer, sir? I mean, was he anybody in particular?'

'Oh, a man named Clough,' my schoolmaster said. 'He's not remembered now. Except for one poem, perhaps. A piece with no title. "Say not the struggle nought availeth" is the opening line. In its marmoreal way it's a good poem. In fact you've given me an idea. We'll make it the next one for repetition.'

I duly learnt the poem. He was a man who insisted upon such things. And I liked it. It was my introduction to Clough. By now of course the poem has wide fame. Churchill and Roosevelt quoted it at each other across the Atlantic when our fortunes in World War Two were at their nadir, and for a while the radio waves and the leader columns of the newspapers hummed with it.

> *Say not the struggle nought availeth,*
> *The labour and the wounds are vain,*
> *The enemy faints not, nor faileth,*
> *And as things have been, they remain.*

145

If hopes were dupes, fears may be liars;
  It may be, in yon smoke concealed,
Your comrades chase e'en now the fliers,
  And, but for you, possess the field.

For while the tired waves, vainly breaking,
  Seem here no painful inch to gain,
Far back through creeks and inlets making
  Came, silent, flooding in, the main,

And not by eastern windows only,
  When daylight comes, comes in the light,
In front the sun climbs slow, how slowly,
  But westward, look, the land is bright.

Clough probably wrote it in Rome, in 1849, as he watched the troops of Garibaldi engaging themselves in an unequal struggle against the forces of reaction, the besieging French under Oudinot, helped by the Austrians and the Neapolitans. It has Clough's fortitude. It has the spare, undecorated quality that Clough was master of and that stemmed from his love and understanding of the poets of the Greek Anthology. But for all that it isn't really typical. You get the same attitude expressed in *Peschiera*, written a little later, with its Tennysonian echo:

'Tis better to have fought and lost
Than never to have fought at all

but none the less it is, with him, a note rarely sounded. When it comes to fighting for causes he identifies himself more often with Claude in *Amours de Voyage*:

Now supposing the French or the Neapolitan soldier
Should by some evil chance come exploring the Maison Serny
(Where the family English are all to assemble for safety),
Am I prepared to lay down my life for the British female?...

Oh, and of course you will say, 'When the time comes, you will
  be ready.'
Ah, but before it comes, am I to presume it will be so?
What I cannot feel now, am I to suppose that I shall feel?
Am I not free to attend for the ripe and indubious instinct?

146

Am I forbidden to wait for the clear and lawful perception?
Is it the calling of man to surrender his knowledge and insight
For the mere venture of what may, perhaps, be the virtuous
action?

Still, I could at any rate see what my schoolmaster meant when he had used the word 'marmoreal', and perhaps the wry, deflationary self-analysis of *Amours de Voyage* would have been less to my taste. I was at the age when I enjoyed reading a poet who could be 'prophetic' and who could make inspiring noises. 'Say not the struggle' was heartening, invigorating stuff. And yet my schoolmaster had said, 'He's not remembered now.' This remark, made in the late 'twenties, was a perfectly accurate statement of how things stood with Clough at that time. His reputation had gone.

And yet when he died, the elite amongst his contemporaries somehow knew that a man of alpha quality had left the stage with the play far from played out. Nothing about Clough is more remarkable than the way in which these people—Carlyle, Temple, Emerson, Froude—were certain about this big, slow-moving man, running a little to fat, flitting from unglamorous job to unglamorous job, quite failing to make his mark in any sort of tangible, demonstrable sense. The poems of *Ambarvalia* and *The Bothie* were in England the only published evidence of talent; even the *Amours* were only known to a small circle of New England readers of Boston's *Atlantic Monthly*. Yet none of this seemed to matter. John Addington Symonds, an undergraduate at Balliol at the time of Clough's death, recalled how he went to Jowett for a tutorial, and was received by a mourning Master with these words: 'I cannot hear your essay this evening, Mr Symonds. I have just heard that Clough is dead.'

It is true that, for a quarter of a century between about 1905 and 1930, his light went very dim indeed; but up till 1900 he was known, respected, and in a restricted circle, read. Before Victoria died Mrs Clough's 1869 edition of her husband's work had been reprinted fourteen times.

It is none the less true that the Victorian reading public never took him to its heart in the way that Tennyson, or even Browning, were taken. It was a generation that took delight (as I did as a schoolboy) in the prophetic vein, where poetry was concerned, in sonorous exhortation, and in hearty sermonising of the kind provided in Browning's 'Rabbi Ben Ezra'. Except for 'Say Not the Struggle', and for brief moments elsewhere, Clough could offer little in this line.

And the people who lived and read during those forty years between his death and the death of the Queen found him lacking in another, more important, respect. His poetry is hard and dry and wry. He has no singing-robes to put on. He is never lush. Small wonder that Swinburne, in whom lushness was a spreading disease, found his work so repugnant. You look in vain in him for opulence of phrase and splendour of image. Rich brocades, stained-glass windows shedding a warm purpureal glow, flowers in fullness and diversity of bloom and heady with scent, languorous rhythms in which melancholy and mortality improbably acquire a sleepy deliciousness ('And after many a summer dies the swan')— Clough turned his back on all of this. Even Matthew Arnold lamented, as has been already noted, 'the deficiency of the *beautiful* in your poems'.

Was this the explanation of what some have seen as an estrangement between Clough and Matthew Arnold? I do not myself believe that there was ever any real estrangement. Arnold writes: 'pray remember that I am and always shall be, whatever I do or say, powerfully attracted towards you, and vitally connected with you: this I am sure of: the period of my development (God forgive me the damned expression) coincides with that of my friendship with you so exactly that I am for ever linked with you by intellectual bonds—the strongest of all: more than you are with me: for your development was really over before you knew me, and you had properly speaking come to your assiette for life.' Arnold goes on to say how he thinks Clough has gone wrong: 'you could never finally as it seemed—"resolve to be thyself"—but were looking for this and that experience, and doubting whether you ought not to adopt this or that mode of being of persons *qui ne vous valaient pas* because it might possibly be nearer the truth than your own...your morbid conscientiousness—you are the most conscientious man I ever knew: but on some lines morbidly so, and it spoils your action.' Though there is subtle and in some ways just criticism of Clough here, this is surely not the language of estrangement. And a little later that same year (on May 1, 1853) Arnold writes 'I do not think I have increased your stock of happiness. You have, however, on the whole, added to mine.' Mr

148

Lionel Trilling, in his admirable book on Matthew Arnold, makes much of the idea that Clough and Arnold became lost to each other. 'The long sad battle with Clough,' he says, 'is fought under a cloak of aesthetic discussion. Arnold does not like Clough's poetry and tells him so, now mitigating his criticism, now roaring it out with humorous exaggeration: Clough, he says, has mistaken the whole method and function of poetry.' And again: '[Arnold] feared his friends and kept them off—feared even Clough at times nearly as much as any of them and as early as 1848 considered attenuating the friendship. He gave up the idea at the time but the relationship certainly grew less and less fertile until by 1853 it was an affectionate formality. "Thyrsis" is the lament for a dead friend but also for a dead friendship.' This, I think, is to make altogether too much of a friendly disagreement between writers about a writing matter. No two poets in our language were ever closer than Arnold and Clough; I believe that closeness and deep affection—made, inevitably perhaps, as the years went by to appear less intense because a man gets married, and has children, and has responsibilities crowding in on him—remained to the end. In August 1859, when Clough had only a little over two years left, Arnold was writing: 'My dear old soul, I find that, au fond, when I compose anything, I care more, still, for your opinion than that of anyone else about it.' This is not the language of a dead friendship.

But there can be no question that Clough's 'unbeautifulness', his 'unpoeticalness', did grate upon many, if not most, of his generation. The fourteen editions up to 1902 notwithstanding, Clough was read with puzzled respect rather than with acclaim.

Then came three decades of almost total neglect. The single voice—one well worth listening to—of J. I. Osborne was raised in a book published in 1920. But that was all. John Drinkwater wrote a book on Victorian poetry in the middle twenties, and, in 187 pages, devoted two sentences to Clough under an astonishing general heading of 'Some Tennysonians'; 'Men like Clough, Dixon, de Tabley were fine spirits finely touched to song,' he says. 'Clough, to speculate idly, with a little more energy, might have found his way into the great group of his age.' The words spread themselves across the page like the perfunctory smile of greeting to a caller scarcely known. In fact, Arnold's complaint about his 'unpoeticalness' went on being accepted as valid, so that we have the irony—Clough himself would have appreciated it—of his greatest friend's becoming the engineer of his total eclipse. The Georgians failed to bear in mind that Arnold, stimulating and original enough as a formulator of general critical principles, could go badly astray in his judgment of individual writers. (Sir Edmund Chambers, academic literary pontiff *par excellence*, has some characteristically dismissive words on Arnold's limitations as a guide up the slopes of Parnassus: 'I do not think he was ever at his best in attempting to expound the fundamental basis of poetic activity.') And by 1910—one has to put the date so far forward because the almost indestructible Florence Nightingale survived till then—there was nobody left alive who had known Clough with sufficient intimacy to put them right.

Yet now, in 1968, Clough's poems have appeared for the first time in the Oxford Editions of Standard Authors. We have never in this country been infected—if that is the word—by the French passion for Pantheons and Academies. Except for a cluttered and oddly haphazard Poets' Corner in Westminster Abbey, we can look for no outward and visible signs whereby a writer may be recognised as having, dead or alive, made the grade. But inclusion in the Oxford Editions of Standard Authors certainly means recognition. For a writer it means either that what he has written has a quality giving it permanent currency, or else it means—this admittedly is more rare—that what he has to say has greater relevance and significance to succeeding generations that it had for his own. One thinks of Stendhal's confident prediction that he would be read in 1880 (though in fact of course he had to wait even longer than that), of Henry James's lament about his insurmountable unsaleability, and of Blake's remaining 'hid' (even though, perhaps, of his own choice). The miracle of resurrection is certainly far from impossible with writers. Indeed the less resounding the initial success the more feasible resurrection seems to become. A contemporary reviewer of Martin Tupper said: 'He has won for himself the vacant throne waiting for him amidst the immortals.' He was even seriously tipped to join Tennyson in the peerage; he was sufficiently sure of this himself that he had coronets enamelled on to his dinner plates so as to be absolutely ready when the big moment came. Then suddenly people began to laugh at his *Proverbial Philosophy*; and then, after the laughter had died down, Tupper plunged into the irreversible oblivion which is the fate of most of us.

The slow revival of interest in Clough dates from around 1930, though doubts about him still continued to be expressed after that date, and he is still far from having reached the comfortable stage of total acceptance. It hasn't yet occurred to the examiners who prescribe the books for reading in English at A Level to put down *Amours de Voyage* or *The Bothie*, but nothing is more certain than that the suggestion will—sooner rather than later—be made.

What are these doubts? Well, they say, for one thing, his output was small. And then there is the worry about what is thought of as his maimed and stunted personality. He was, not so much the boy who never grew up as the boy who grew up too soon. Admirable of course his refusal ever to truckle in the way any man with a career in mind almost inevitably has to; yet, having struck off alone across country where there was no trodden path, doesn't he somehow lack the fibre and guts to compel, through force of character and quality of utterance, the attention of the world, so that even if it won't turn his way it will follow his progress with understanding and engrossed attention?

What substance is there in any of this? Think first of his output. For a man who died at forty-two it wasn't as meagre as all that. The 1951 edition of his poems by Lowry, Mulhauser and Norrington runs to 456 pages; the 'prose remains', excluding of course the letters, occupy 138 pages of Blanche Clough's edition of 1888. An American scholar, Walter E. Houghton, has been at pains to count the lines in the Clough definitive edition above mentioned and those in the 1950 edition of Matthew Arnold's *Poetical Works* edited by Lowry and Tinker. The computation comes out at 13,578 for Clough and 14,023 for Arnold. A damned close-run thing, in fact. Arnold's prose is of course infinitely more various and extensive than Clough's, but, thinking of them both as poets (and I am not suggesting here that Clough should be thought of as anything else, although his qualities as a letter-writer are very far from negligible), Clough's productivity turns out, surprisingly, to be far higher than Arnold's once the fact that his life-span was shorter than Arnold's by twenty-four years is taken into account. Clough wrote in sudden spurts, with long, quiescent gaps in between, but when the fit was on him he wrote fast. The demon drove. *The Bothie*, a rich and complicated poem of nearly 1,800 lines, was written in a few intense weeks during the autumn of 1848. On September 4, 1848, he writes to Tom Arnold: 'I believe I shall probably in about six weeks' time publish conjointly with Burbidge a volume of poems [this was of course *Ambarvalia*]. Some of them I hope you will like; but I don't think much will come of it. I don't much intend writing any more verse.' Yet on October 23, seven weeks later, he is able to inform his sister: '*My* little book [that is, *The Bothie*] I hope, will be out in ten days.' This little sentence gives proof of concentrated creative energy of a very high order. Is this an *indolent* man, full of self-mistrust and uncertain of his direction?

What of the second, far more serious complaint, that his work is negative and colourless and that it must always fail because of this to illuminate, to excite, to enforce attention? Must Beatrice's gibe at Benedick 'Nobody heeds you' always be applied to him?

I suggest that Clough is being heeded, and that he is going to be heeded more and more. What the Victorians, although obscurely aware of the greatness of the man, misunderstood in him, or what they found strange and foreign to their conception of how life should be lived and poems written; what the generation between 1902 and 1930 took as unread, we are today finding both exciting and relevant to our situation and to our needs.

Our age is one of separateness and profound mistrust. We consider that the attitudes have all been struck. The emperors have all strutted by, and the fact that they none of them had any clothes on has by this time become so commonplace as scarcely to deserve mention. And action too, as opposed to outward display and bombast, even heroic action—the kind Carlyle spilt so much ink over—leads also, people are beginning ruefully to say, to tragedy and loss and a mockery of achievement.

Clough's predominant mood and attitude chime with this feeling which we are familiar with, but which the Victorians felt far less strongly and which, even when they did feel it, they strenuously suppressed.

> Hope evermore and believe, O man, for e'en as thy thought
> So are the things that thou see'st; e'en as thy hope and belief.
> Cowardly art thou and timid? they rise to provoke thee against them;
> Hast thou courage? enough, see them exulting to yield.

For Clough the conceptions of hope and belief cannot and must not ever be generalised; they have reality only for the self; their validity is only for the self. They are like a couple of rag dolls which may reasonably represent a prince and a princess—but for one particular small child only. No harm at all in hope or belief, Clough seems to be saying. Indeed they may be necessary just as the rag-doll is to the toddler, but—and Clough is insistent here— we must recognise them for what they are.

Who can doubt that this is a line of thought which evokes a wide response today? The Victorians took less kindly to it, and it is easy to see why. They were robust and practical. They had a strong disinclination to be fobbed off with dusty answers when they themselves were so hot for certainties. And after all, did not their huge success in public affairs, their top-of-the-charts standing in the world at large, provide them with the unfailing reassurance that they, if any generation ever, had earned the right to be positive in their affirmations? 'Though without much fame, he had no envy.' So Bagehot wrote of Clough in an essay which is full of appreciativeness and discernment. Yet for all that one catches, in a sentence such as this, the puzzlement of a highly intelligent Victorian when applying himself to the enigma of Clough. I find in Bagehot's words a hint, perhaps unintentional and unconscious, of an exasperated question: Why can't this dear man, outstandingly able as we know him to be, so formidable an intellect that sometimes even someone like Matthew Arnold appears like a garrulous schoolboy beside him—why can't he manage to be a bit more like the rest of us?

Something else that makes us heed him is that very quality— the 'deficiency of the beautiful'—which worried Matthew Arnold so much. We like a certain flatness and dryness in our poetry. The florid, the exuberant, the excessively detailed don't nowadays find much favour (it is true that modern poetry in general sets great store by the image, and Clough, admittedly is no man for images; but these images that we love must be concentrated and single. Proliferation of images in the Shakespearean manner is not the modern way).

Clough's style is sober and simple in vocabulary, often syntactic-ally dense, often idiomatic and colloquial. He was always searching —and we find the search exciting—for that elusive equilibrium between thought and style. As he said in an unpublished lecture, he always mistrusted 'thinking of the words rather than the thought, and running off upon the casualties of the form of an expression instead of moving on with the essential tendency of the thought'. A remark like this serves to account for one of the greatest pleasures of his poetry: its syntactical strength:

> *Blessed are those who have not seen,*
> *And who have yet believed*
> *The witness, here that has not been,*
> *From heaven they have received.*
> *Blessed are those who have not known*
> *The things that stand before them,*
> *And for a vision of their own*
> *Can piously ignore them.*
> *So let me think whate'er befall,*
> *That in the city duly*
> *Some men there are who love at all,*
> *Some women who love truly;*
> *And that upon two million odd*
> *Transgressors in sad plenty,*
> *Mercy will of a gracious God*
> *Be shown—because of twenty.*

Or there is this, one of the *Seven Sonnets*, which comes from the (B) Notebook of 1851 and which is probably not a final draft:

> *But if, as (not by what the soul desired*
> *Swayed in the judgment) wisest men have thought,*
> *And (furnishing the evidence it sought)*
> *Man's heart hath ever fervently required,*
> *And story, for that reason deemed inspired,*
> *To every clime, in every age, hath taught;*
> *If in this human complex there be aught*
> *Not lost in death, as not in birth acquired,*
> *O then, though cold the lips that did convey*
> *Rich freights of meaning, dead each living sphere*
> *Where thought abode and fancy loved to play,*
> *Thou, yet we think, somewhere somehow still art,*
> *And satisfied with that the patient heart*
> *The where and how doth not desire to hear.*

He is nearly always wonderfully at home in the colloquial, quick-moving manner. He can even, as has already been seen in these pages, massage the stiff muscles of the hexameter form into conversational suppleness. Using a wide variety of rhythms, he can achieve the same effects in the Spirit's mockeries in *Dipsychus*:

> *This world is very odd, we see;*
>   *We do not comprehend it;*
> *But in one fact can all agree*
>   *God won't, and we can't mend it.*

Or:

> *Submit, submit!*
> *For tell me then, in earth's great laws*
> *Have you found any saving clause,*
> *Exemption special granted you*
> *From doing what the rest must do?*
> *Of Common Sense who made you quit,*
> *And told you, you'd no need of it,*
> *Nor to submit?*

Or, again in the mouth of the Spirit, the blank-verse self-scourgings he administers in lines like:

> *Or you'll perhaps teach youth (I do not question*
> *Some downward turn you may find, some evasion*
> *Of the broad highway's glaring wide ascent),*
> *Teach youth—in a small way; that is, always*
> *So as to have much time left for yourself;*
> *This you can't sacrifice, your leisure's precious.*
> *Heartily you will not take to anything;*
> *Will parents like that, think you? 'He writes poems,*
> *He's odd opinions—hm!—and's not in Orders'—*
> *For that you won't be. Well, old college fame,*
> *The charity of some free-thinking merchant,*
> *Or friendly intercession brings a first pupil;*
> *And not a second. Oh, or if it should,*
> *Whatever happen, don't I see you still,*
> *Living no life at all? Even as now*
> *An o'ergrown baby, sucking at the dugs*
> *Of Instinct, dry long since. Come, come, you are old enough*
> *For spoon-meat surely.*

Submit! This is the central imperative in Clough's life. He

doesn't want to be exempted from doing what the rest must do because separateness and loneliness are the corollaries of any such exemption, and these must always be hard for human frailty to bear. But his intelligence and his sense of personal integrity link hands to keep him away from the submission and submergence which he craves. In other words, Clough is obsessed with the question of commitment, and this too is something which gives his work meaningful vitality for the modern reader because commitment is a central preoccupation for writers of our time. The feeling that we have passed our apprenticeship and that it is time we set up in business on our own—each one his own God the Father Almighty—is of course stronger now, more urgent, more general, than it was in Clough's time. We have, after all, managed to create real genuine, dazzling, close-quarters suns for ourselves, and the Greeks long ago had no difficulty at all in thinking of Apollo as a God. But like Clough we hesitate. We still want, like children in the dark, to hold hands—to become Comrades in the Marxist sense so that Action, the word that so tormented Clough, ceases to be an anguished personal matter, but instead is something mindless and reassuring, something dealt with by the Action Committee. Or, if not Marxists, then Humanists or Existentialists, or at any rate—this is really the essential thing— something *plural* so that we may enjoy the reassurance of never having to go it quite alone. Clough thought hard and long about this and made memorable poetry out of his dilemma. 'A kidnapped child of Heaven' he calls himself in a vivid phrase which epitomises a human situation perhaps more familiar to us than it was even to him.

Clough can't commit himself, or rather he can't commit himself in any crucial, *exposed* way; he is not disposed to take the lead in any sort of commitment, but only willing to be biddable, to carry out orders in 'other ranks' capacity. In this century, T. E. Lawrence's need to turn himself into a submerged Aircraftman Shaw is a parallel to the need of Clough.

'...*were the end ours*,'

he says in the character of Dipsychus,

'*One's choice and the correlative of soul,*
To drudge were then sweet service. But indeed

156

The earth moves slowly, if it moves at all,
And by the general, not the single force.
At the (huge) members of the vast machine,
In all those crowded rooms of industry,
No individual soul has loftier leave
Than fiddling with a piston or a valve.
Well, one could bear that also: one could drudge
And do one's petty part, and be content
In base manipulation, solaced still
By thinking of the leagued fraternity,
And of co-operation, and the effect
Of the great engine. If indeed it work,
And is not a mere treadmill! Which it may be;
Who can confirm it is not? We ask Action,
And dream of arms and conflict; and string up
All self-devotion's muscles; and are set
To fold up papers. To what end? We know not.
Other folks do so; it is always done;
And it perhaps is right. And we are paid for it.
For nothing else we can be. He that eats
Must serve; and serve as other servants do:
And don the lacquey's livery of the house.
Oh, could I shoot my thoughts up to the sky,
A column of pure shape, for all to observe!—
But I must slave, a meagre coral-worm,
To build beneath the tide with excrement
What one day will be island, or be reef,
And will feed men or wreck them. Well, well, well,
Adieu, ye twisted thinkings. I submit.'

Twisted thinkings? Twisted or not, they give incomparable expression to the malaise that enfeebles us here and now in the 1960s. If you substitute 'shop-floor' for 'rooms of industry' the whole passage comes very close indeed.

It isn't surprising, reading such a passage as this, to find that Clough, a hundred-odd years before he gained general currency, is the creator of the anti-hero. Claude in *Amours de Voyage* is of course his greatest success in this line, and it's important to emphasise that Claude is a genuine creation in the novelistic sense—a bodying forth of something outside, independent of, the

157

self. Claude is not simply Clough, as Dipsychus is. Of course there are Cloughian elements in him; all character-creation after all has to be built up out of the self. But in Claude Clough is isolating the particularly anti-heroic elements he sees in himself, giving them emphasis, and introducing an element of self-mockery. But only an element. There are moments—longish ones—when his honesty compels him to recognise an inescapable rightness in Claude's cynical rejection of the role of hero.

'I will go where I am led, and will not dictate to the chances.'

This comes near the end of the poem, and we recognise at last a kind of stoic heroism in the anti-heroics.

Edmund too in 'The Clergyman's First Tale' from *Mari Magno*, is the anti-hero in love. Claude would have had no use for the softer, more muted tones in which he expresses himself, but he makes up his mind, and then unmakes it, in exactly the same way as his predecessor:

> *Would I could wish my wishes all to rest,*
> *And know to wish the wish that were the best!*
> *O for some winnowing wind, to the empty air*
> *This chaff of easy sympathies to bear*
> *Far off, and leave me of myself aware!...*
>
> *Why do I wait? what more propose to know?*
> *Where the sweet mandate bids me, let me go;*
> *My conscience in my impulse let me find,*
> *Justification in the moving mind,*
> *Law in the strong desire...*

(Who, after that, could claim that existentialism came in with Sartre?)

In his itch for self-submergence, for anonymity, I have likened him to T. E. Lawrence. It might at first glance seem fanciful to see him as someone who prefigures significantly the other, greater Lawrence. Yet think of this passage from *A Propos of 'Lady Chatterley's Lover'*: 'The body's life is the life of sensations and emotions. The body feels real hunger, real thirst, real joy in the sun or the snow, real pleasure in the smell of roses or the look of a lilac-bush; real anger, real sorrow, real love, real tenderness, real warmth, real passion, real hate, real grief. All the emotions

158

belong to the body, and are only recognised by the mind.' Is it really so bizarre to imagine Clough responding to such a passage as this? All his upbringing, all the stringent intellectual disciplines of his life at Rugby, all those inhibitions bred up in him by reason of his having been born in an age when the body's life had been driven underground, condemned to irrevocable exile: all these inescapable Cloughian facts proclaim the absurdity of any such response. Yet 'the buried life', the 'hidden self'—how obsessed by them he is, how he longs to bring them up into the light of day for an airing. *Dipsychus* is about nothing if it isn't about this, and '*Natura Naturans*'—the poem that so shocked Blanche—has Lawrentian as well as Emersonian undertones. Of course Dipsychus takes a high moral tone with the quips and needlings of his Spirit-familiar, but can it not be effectively argued that Clough, like Milton, was (to give him a loaded name) 'of the Devil's party without knowing it'?

'*Come, my pretty boy,*'

the Spirit tells him,

> '*You have been making mows to the blank sky*
> *Quite long enough for good. We'll put you up*
> *Into the higher form. 'Tis time you learn*
> *The Second Reverence, for things around.*
> *Up, then, and go amongst them; don't be timid;*
> *Look at them quietly a bit: by-and-by*
> *Respect will come, and healthy appetite...*'

Perhaps this plea for a great, if greatly flawed, writer is best brought to a close with yet one more quotation from Matthew Arnold, the friend who loved him, who misunderstood him, and who, in *Thyrsis*, unwittingly did his reputation harm. This time the quotation will be, not from Arnold's letters to Clough (these too, of course, in their delayed time-bomb fashion tended to strengthen doubts about him) but from Arnold's most famous sonnet, the one on Shakespeare. 'We ask and ask,' says Arnold, and further on, 'thou...Didst walk the earth unguessed at.'

No one of course is going to say that in Clough we have an undiscovered Shakespeare on our hands. Yet he is mysterious; he keeps his secrets still. He stimulates our curiosity, invites our questions. Was that lament of Florence Nightingale's true, and, if true, in what sense: 'Oh Jonathan, my brother Jonathan, my love for thee was very great, PASSING THE LOVE OF WOMEN.' What exactly did he die of? Scarlatina? Unlikely. Malaria? For a strong man in the prime of life still more unlikely. Was it a death-wish, admitted to himself but to no one besides? The scribbling-against-time at *Mari Magno* and the inexpugnable melancholy he inherited from Anne Perfect support the idea. Was his determination to let things happen to him, to refuse to mould and shape his existence towards a chosen end, the result of a deliberate making-up of his mind, the expression of a buttoned-up, private purposefulness? Or was it simply a case of *laissez-aller*, a symptom of indolence and exhaustion?

There can be no doubt that he was pressed too hard at Rugby, that Thomas Arnold stretched him till he almost broke; there can be no doubt either that he inherited lethargy, as well as melancholy, from his mother. But there was immense purposefulness in him too, and hardness of mind, and integrity. How characteristic of him is the grim, dogged little note he wrote to the Council of University Hall on October 30, 1851, after it had asked him for suggestions about how the number of students might be increased. 'The Principal in compliance with a resolution of the Committee of Management at their meeting on Tuesday last has to state to the Chairman of the Council that he is unable to offer any suggestion to the Council in the present occasion. No measure that he can think of would, he believes, have more than a very gradual effect in the way of increasing the number of students. He has only to add that the conduct of the twelve Students now resident has been perfectly good and correct.' No wonder the lonely, unco-operative Principal of University Hall, Gower Street was such a worry to his governing body, to Crabb Robinson and his like, who played, and judged, the career game according to rules as standard then as now. He was, of course, no eccentric, no wild one, even though he admired Byron and the influence of Byron's writing on him was strong. He bowed—somewhat stiffly perhaps, but he bowed—in all the appropriate situations. He was too fond of fluctuating, as Matthew Arnold shrewdly said. (Though it must be remembered that Arnold also said, about himself, 'For me, I am a reed, a very whoreson Bullrush.')

Yet, in the end, the pattern of his life—the inner pattern, the secret pattern—was a willed one. The outward appearance of a sickly self-questioner being pushed around is deceptive. He was his own man always. And Blanche, no more than anybody else, could ever exactly see how that was. He preserved his integrity in private ways which took no account of the gambits and routines by which people in charge—or perhaps not in charge—of their personal situations are judged. Look hard at him. Look long at him. And what finally you come to see is an heroic, and not a defeated, figure. What lines, out of all his 13,000-odd would he like us best to remember him by? These, I think: so let them make their affirmation once again:

> *But play no tricks upon thy soul, O man;*
> *Let fact be fact, and life the thing it can.*

A Select Reading List

Poems and Prose Remains of A.H.C. 2 Vols. London, 1869
Prose Remains with a Selection from his Letters and a Memoir by his wife. London, 1888
The Correspondence of A.H.C. Edited Frederick L. Mulhauser. Oxford, 1957
Poems of A.H.C. Edited Lowry, Norrington and Mulhauser. Oxford, 1951
The Poems of A.H.C. Edited A. L. P. Norrington. Oxford Editions of Standard Authors 1968

Letters of Matthew Arnold & A.H.C. Edited Lowry. Oxford, 1932
William Allingham: A.H.C. *Fraser's Magazine*, October 1866
Walter Bagehot: A.H.C. (Literary Studies, Vol. 2. London, 1895)
Katharine Chorley: A.H.C. The Uncommitted Mind. Oxford, 1962
R. W. Church: A.H.C. *The Christian Remembrancer*, January 1863
Walter Houghton: *The Poetry of Clough*. Yale, 1963
R. H. Hutton: A.H.C. (Literary Essays). London, 1888
Goldie Levy: A.H.C. London, 1938
F. L. Lucas: 'Thyrsis'. *Life and Letters*, May 1929
Paula Lutonsky: A.H.C. Wiener Beiträge zur Englischen Philologie 1912
Desmond MacCarthy: A.H.C. in *Portraits*. London, 1931
James I. Osborne: A.H.C. Constable. London, 1920
Henry Sidgwick: A.H.C. in *Miscellaneous Essays and Addresses*. London, 1904
Leslie Stephen: A.H.C. in *Dictionary of National Biography*
J. A. Symonds: 'Last and First'. *Fortnightly Review*. December 1868
Samuel Waddington: A.H.C. A Monograph. London, 1883
Humbert Wolfe: A.H.C. in *The 1860s*. Cambridge, 1932
Frances J. Woodward: A.H.C. in *The Doctor's Disciples*. Oxford, 1954

Paul Veyriras: A.H.C. Didier. Paris, 1964

Thomas Arnold the younger: Article in *The Christian Remembrancer*. January 1898. *New Zealand Letters*. Ed. J. Bertram. Auckland and OUP, 1966
Henri Brémond: *L'Inquiétude Religieuse*. Paris, 1930
B. A. Clough: *A Memoir of Anne Jemima Clough*. London, 1903
Edward T. Cook: *Life of Florence Nightingale*. London, 1913
H. Crabb Robinson: *Books and their Writers*. Ed. Edith Morley. London, 1938
W. H. Dunn: *J. A. Froude*. Oxford, 1961
R. W. Emerson: *Journals 1820–72*. Cambridge, Massachussetts, 1912
J. A. Froude: *T. Carlyle: A History of his Life in London 1834–81*. London, 1884
J. D. Jump: *Matthew Arnold*. London, 1955
William Knight: *Principal Shairp and his Friends*. London, 1888
W. C. Lake: *Rugby and Oxford 1830–1850*
C. E. Norton: *Letters*. London, 1903
J. C. Shairp: 'Balliol Scholars' article in *Macmillan's Magazine*. March 1873
A. P. Stanley: *Life of Thomas Arnold*. London, 1944
A. C. Tait: *Life by Davidson and Benham*. London, 1891
Memoirs of Archbishop Temple. Ed. Sandford. London, 1906
Kathleen Tillotson: 'Rugby 1850', *Review of English Studies*. April 1953
Lionel Trilling; *Matthew Arnold*. London, 1939
Mrs Humphrey Ward: *A Writer's Recollections*. London, 1918
Wilfrid Ward: *W. G. Ward and the Oxford Movement*. London, 1889
Basil Willey: *19th Century Studies*. London, 1949
C. Woodham Smith: *Florence Nightingale*. London, 1951
G. M. Young: *Portrait of an age; Victorian England*. Oxford, 1936

Index

Clough, A. H.—*continued*
120; Clerk to the Privy Council, 121; Tour of continent as secretary to a Commission, 1856, 122; Marriage, 1854, 123; At St Mark's Crescent, Regent's Park, 123; Children, 123; Florence Nightingale's unpaid assistant, 126–32; Illness, 131; Journey to Greece, 133; *Mari Magno*, 133–9; Journey to France and Italy, 140–4; Death, 144; *Say Not the Struggle*, 145–7; His fluctuating reputation, 147–51; His output, 151; His relevance today, 152–3; His style, 153–5; His obsession with the question of commitment, 156–8; His resemblance to the two Lawrences; 158–9; His melancholy, 160
Coleridge, J. T., 19
Coleridge, Samuel Taylor, 57
Crabbe, George, 135, 138
Crimean War, 122, 128

Dana, Richard Henry, 116
'Decade', the, 53
Derby, Lord, 105, 117
Dickens, Charles, 121
Doyle, F. H., 33
Drinkwater, John, 149
Dwights, the, 109

Emerson, Ralph Waldo, 56–9, 63, 70, 72, 73, 89, 101, 104, 109, 111, 122, 123, 124, 128, 135, 140, 147

Felton, Cornelius Conway, 116
Fields, James Thomas, 116
Froude, James Anthony, 37, 58, 80, 93, 94, 147
Free Soilers, 109
Fuller, Margaret, 83, 110

Garibaldi, Giuseppe, 81, 82, 146
Gaskell, Elizabeth Cleghorn, 80
Gell, J. P., 25, 27, 39, 43, 52, 53
Gladstone, William Ewart, 126
Goethe, Johann Wolfgang von, 102, 103
Gosse, Sir Edmund, 31
Granville, Lord, 117, 118, 121

Hall, Dr John, 128
Hampden, Renn Dickson, 56

Hawkins, Edward. Provost of Oriel, 56, 57, 79, 89, 103
Herbert, Sidney, 126, 127, 129, 130, 141
Houghton, W. E., 151
Housman, A. E., 113
Howe, Estes, 109, 116
Howes, Mrs, 111
Hudson, George. 'The Railway King', 54
Hughes, Tom, 22, 32, 33
Hutton, R. H., 104

James, Henry, 91, 125, 150
Jewsbury, Geraldine, 80
Jowett, Benjamin. Master of Balliol, 31, 54, 133, 147

Keble, John, 37
Kingsley, Charles, 125

Lake, W. C. Dean of Durham, 19, 29, 123
Lamartine, Alphonse de, 70, 81
Lansdowne, Lord, 68
Lawrence, D. H., 64, 158
Lawrence, T. E., 158
Lee, John Prince, 20
Longfellow, Henry Wadsworth, 108, 110, 116
Lingen, Robert, 117
Lowell, James Russell, 84, 107, 109, 110, 111, 116, 124
Lowry, H. F., 151
Lucas, F. L., 90
Lyell, Sir Charles, 109

Macaulay, Lord, 124
Macmillan's Magazine, 120
MacNeill, Sir John, 132
Mai, Aunt (Florence Nightingale's), 104
Martineau, Richard, 94
Masson, David, 120
Mazzini, Giuseppe, 81, 83, 84, 94
Milnes, Richard Monckton, 128
Mohl, Madame, 126, 140
Mulhauser, F. L., 151

Napoleon, Louis, 81
Newman, John Henry, Cardinal, 34, 37, 38, 52, 53, 69

Nightingale, Florence, 34, 103, 104, 123, 126, 127, 128, 129, 130, 131, 133, 140, 141, 143, 159
Norrington, Sir Arthur, 151
North American Review, 113
North British Review, 131
Norton, C. E., 63, 110, 115, 116, 121, 122, 123, 124, 125, 134, 143
Novara, Battle of, 81

Osborne, J. I., 67, 68, 149
Oudinot, Nicolas-Charles, Maréchal, 82, 146

Palgrave, Sir Francis, 81, 82, 117, 118
Palmerston, Lord, 140
Panmure, Lord, 122, 129, 130
Patmore, Coventry, 124, 134, 138
Patterdale, 72
Philippe, Louis, 58
Pio Nono, 81, 82
Plutarch, Langhorne's, 124, 125, 126
Price, Bonamy, 20
Prescott, William Hickling, 109, 111
Putnam's Monthly, 113

Quincy, Josiah, 116

Racine, Jean, 81
Robinson, Crabb, 120, 160
Rochefoucauld, Duc de la, 64
Rossi, Pellegrino, 81
Russell, Lord John, 105

Sewell, William. Rector of Exeter College, 58
Shairp, John Campbell, 55, 66, 83, 84, 88, 89, 93, 120
Sidgwick, Henry, 137, 138

Simpkinson, J. N., 24, 44, 51
Smith, Alexander, 113
Smith, Samuel. Father-in-law of AHC, 106, 112, 118, 119, 121
Stanley, A. P., 19, 22, 51, 70
Stendhal (Marie-Henri Beyle), 87, 150
Stowe, H. B., 108
Strachey, Lytton, 21
Sumner, Charles, 109
Swinburne, Algernon Charles, 148
Symonds, J. A., 138, 147

Tait, Archibald Campbell, 50, 54
Temple, Frederick, 32, 33, 37, 117, 118, 119, 121, 147
Tennyson, Alfred Lord, 124, 125, 132, 140, 141, 142, 146, 147, 150
Thackeray, William Makepeace, 77, 107, 108, 110, 112, 116, 121
Thomas, George, 83
Thoreau, Henry David, 110
Ticknor, George, 108, 109, 111
Trilling, Lionel, 149
Trollope, Anthony, 126
Tupper, Martin, 150

Verney, Sir Harry, 140

Walrond, Theodore, 50, 51, 83
Ward, Mrs, 110
Ward, W. G. Fellow of Balliol, 21, 31, 34, 36ff., 46, 52, 53, 68, 69, 105
White, Blanco, 55
Wilson, Dr, 143
Winthrop, Lindell, 111, 112
Woodward, Miss F. J., 68, 88
Wooll, Dr, 17, 18
Wordsworth, William, 73